THE UNBRANDED STUDENT

Reclaiming Your College Search

Dr. Lee Brown

Benjamin P. Roberts

Unbranded Student
North Richland Hills, Texas 76182
www.unbrandedstudent.com

This book is dedicated to every high school student with dreams of going to college.

TABLE OF CONTENTS

INTRODUCTION
(Don't skip this part.)

Welcome to the New Story

If your life were a story, how do you tell the part about going to college?[1] Are you going to the same school the last three generations of your family attended? Have you set your sights on the prestige of an Ivy League school? Are you and your best friend rooming together at a school she picked? Are you a football fan going to your team's school because of the memories you made with your dad on Saturdays watching games?

Our culture tells a story about college too. It goes something like this: If you want to get a good job, you have to earn a degree. And if you want your résumé to stand out, you need to go to a prestigious university. But to get into that university, you have to make yourself as attractive as possible. You need to have activities and awards and accomplishments to play up in your admissions essays. And, as you have been told non-stop, your college years are some of the best of your life! You belong at a school where you can have the best time, be part of the best programs and access the best opportunities.

---

[1] We're assuming that your plan is to go to college. It doesn't have to be. There are great options for your future that might not include a university degree. This book isn't going to be everything to everyone.

Sound familiar? It's like you're expected to be a brand rather than a person. You have to contort yourself to be just the right kind of person you believe this school wants you to be, instead of the person you are—the unique and wonderful person whose hopes and dreams go far beyond the years you will spend in college.

It's a good story, and parts of it ring true. But most of this story is outdated, shortsighted, and filled with downright lies. And that matters to you because if you base your decisions about college on a faulty or incomplete story, it's bound to affect your own life story too. Most of us aren't in the habit of talking about life as if we're living in a story, but isn't that how we think about the events of our past? The decisions you make about college right now will determine the course of your life. In a sense, they'll write your life story. And don't you want it to be a story of a fulfilling, happy, and successful life? You know by now there are no surefire guarantees of happiness and success, but your choices can set you up for a better chance at getting the life you want.

That's what this book is about: We want to tell you a new story. And like any good story, we'll tell you the Five W's: *Who, What, When, Where, Why*. We think you'll like this story. In the old version, the universities have the power—they're the ones who hold the keys and the degrees, and you have to make yourself attractive to get their attention.

But in this new story, you're the one with the power.

Meet the Authors

Who are we to be making such claims? We're Ben and Lee, two guys working in higher education who want to help you make the most of your college experience.

Ben Roberts

I graduated from New York University in 2006 with a Bachelor of Arts and have spent my career working for companies focused on higher education and helping students find their right path. In just the last five years, I have been on over 300 college campuses speaking to presidents and provosts about the best way to help their students graduate. Well, that's not the whole story—one sentence in and I'm already keeping something back. Really, my first job out of college was selling Hondas at a small dealership in Texas—more on this story later. I'm passionate about championing the success of international and first-generation students searching for college. Oh, and I got an MBA from Baylor. Most important are my wife, Sara, and my two kids, Moses and Esther.

Lee Brown

After high school, I attended community college for a year before transferring to a large regional university to get my business degree in 2006. Like any pragmatic newly married husband, I took a secure job with the large financial institution I had interned with during school. As it turned out, I learned during the 2008 recession that those large banks were not as stable and predictable as I thought. While working for the bank, I went to school to get my MBA at night and eventually left the industry to pursue a PhD and a job in academia[2]. I now teach at Texas Woman's University, a large regional university within driving distance to most of my family, and I spend my free time with my wife and kids. My educational history is pretty unusual for academia, which is typically obsessed with the diversity and prestige of a candidate's education, but I had a plan for my college education, and it's worked out well for me so far.

---

[2] Thanks to my wonderful wife who supported me through graduate school while also being an amazing mom to our young kids.

A NOTE
to Parents, Teachers, and Administrators

This new story we mentioned to students in the introduction affects you too. Students are facing huge challenges as they launch their college search. We caution them against the skyrocketing student debt, unused college degrees, and rising dropout rate—just to name a few. To manage these challenges, we need to rethink our approach to the entire college-search process. We currently think about helping our students get to the most prestigious school and pick the major we feel has the biggest earning potential, so they can find the highest paying job upon graduation. That's bad advice. We should be helping students identify the right school for them, declare a major that fits their passions and aptitudes, and find a job that will bring the individual student the most joy and fulfillment. We need to rewrite the current global narrative of a one-size-fits-all path to college so the search process becomes an individual endeavor for each student.

The reality is, where universities once held the power to pick and choose students, they're now working harder than ever to keep up enrollment. The National Student Clearinghouse reports that student enrollment has dropped for five straight years, and not by a little. "There were just over 18 million students enrolled in higher education nationally in the semester just ended [Spring 2017]—2.4 million fewer than there were in the fall of 2011, the most recent peak."[3]

11

This means that students have more power than ever to choose their own path into higher education. We're not talking about easy entry into top-tier universities. We are talking about a new view of what college is and how to get there: Not going to the college their friends are going to. Not going to the college their great-grandfather went to. Not going to the college that will look best on their résumé. And definitely not twisting the facts about themselves and their accomplishments to make a certain university take notice of them. None of these factors are bad in and of themselves, but they expose a way of thinking about college as *the end*. We hope to convince your students that college can be more—it should be a means to an end rather than an end in itself. What good is a degree if it doesn't align with your student's unique identity and help launch them into their life based on their passions?

Our goal is to challenge students to examine their passions, aptitudes, values, and dreams to determine what kinds of schools are the best fit for *them*. When students put all these pieces together, they can take a highly intentional, authentic, and tailored approach to choosing a list of schools that will provide a more fulfilling and successful outcome. They can design an ideal path for the kind of life and career they hope to have beyond their college years.

[3] Jon Marcus, "Universities and colleges struggle to stem big drops in enrollment," The Hechinger Report, June 29, 2017, http://hechingerreport.org/universities-colleges-struggle-stem-big-drops-enrollment/.

Some of you are squirming in your seats right now. You might feel the boat rocking a bit too much. But this book reflects the realities we've seen firsthand through our work in higher education. We've watched these changes happening before our eyes. I (Ben) have sat through countless meetings with college presidents and admissions staff lamenting the drop in enrollment. I (Lee) have watched handfuls of my own students graduate every semester without a plan for how to use their business degree beyond school. College was the goal, and they accomplished it. Now what? They would have been better served if they'd known how to use college as the *tool* to achieve the life they wanted.

We hope you'll hear us out and encourage your students to do the same. You have a significant part to play in this new narrative unfolding in higher education.

1 Let's Start with My Story

So, why this new story about college? What's wrong with the old one?

It's setting students up to fail, and enough people are starting to notice.

Remember that in the old story the universities have the power? That's because in their story, they're the main character, the protagonist. College is the ultimate goal because …

The last three generations of your family went there!

You're going to school with your best friends!

Attending an Ivy League school is how you define yourself!

The End.

Do you see the problem?

This might work if the story were about college. But your life story isn't just about college, is it? Your story goes on from there—hopefully, to wonderful and fulfilling things in the years beyond university. In that story, *you're the main character*. You're the protagonist. I'll say it again because it sounds so good: You're the one with the power.

Let me show you something. I think a visual aid might help.

If you could sum up the old story in a graphic, it would look something like this:

THE INVERTED PYRAMID
OF GOOD INTENTIONS

You get into that school you were so excited about, and then, oh geez, you have to pick a **major**. It isn't the first time you've thought about it, but the major wasn't your primary concern—it was more about the college and the experience you wanted. Then you hit your senior year in college, and start to think, *Oh no, I'm going to have to get a job*, so you scramble to figure out what kind of job you can get with your major.

Then, you get out into the world and maybe through a couple years in that first job, but you start to wonder:

*What's my **purpose**?*

Why am I doing this?

Who am I really?

And by your late twenties, you suddenly feel you've built your identity upside down. Do you know what happens when you build a pyramid upside down? The slightest breath of wind can topple it. What are examples of wind-toppling events? Not finding the right job as soon as you graduate, getting fired from your first job, realizing the job you dreamed of is an awful slog.

THE TOPPLED PYRAMID OF GOOD INTENTIONS

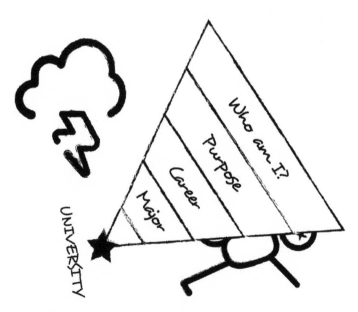

Do you want to set yourself up for the storms of life to crush you under the weight of your unfulfilled dreams? No, of course you don't. This is why we need a new story. This is how the old story is failing thousands of students. And we don't want you to be one of them.

Like I said before, this isn't just theory. I know this is true because it happened to me (Ben). I failed. I got roughed up by the storms of life because I built my pyramid upside down, and it started with a shortsighted view of college. Let me tell you what happened.

Sara Gets Her Degree

My story starts with my wife, Sara. I met Sara at a weekend retreat when we were both fifteen. Sara caught my eye the first time I saw her, and my reaction was a subtle mumbled "hubba hubba" in the misogynistic custom of the early 2000s—be better than me, young men and women. Three months after meeting her, I confessed it was our shared destiny to be married. Like any fifteen-year-old would react, she was thrilled by my declaration of love!

Not really. She smiled and said I liked the idea of her but not really her and that we could be the best of friends. I think she stole that line from Nathaniel Hawthorne's *The Scarlet Letter*. In the end, I was right! Almost two decades later, we are married and have two children.

Sara dreamed of going to a prestigious private university several states away, but her parents—who had attended community college and trade schools off and on—did not approve. Their point of view was that an education was an education, so why not try to save money? Sara was only aware of two options when it came to college: big, expensive schools that seemed impossible to get into, and the local school everyone was accepted to out of high school. Because she was denied the former, she went to the latter.

At the local university, she felt like a number being pushed through a rote program that didn't serve to accomplish any of her goals. She felt uninspired and was being challenged in all the wrong areas. (Instead of struggling through how to acclimate to a new town or how to get along with a funky-smelling first-year roommate, Sara was in a crummy apartment ten minutes from the house she grew up in and working full-time to pay for it.) Her mindset shifted. She didn't feel like she was working toward a bright and rewarding future; she was just figuring out the best way to survive her present misery. She did what a lot of students do when they don't see a light at the end of the tunnel: she dropped out of school, worked full-time as a waitress, and performed in a few local plays.

Sara fell prey to college branding and assumptions she had about school based on her lack of guidance. Like a lot of students, she incorrectly thought schools were either caviar or tuna. She couldn't afford caviar, and she didn't want tuna, so she went hungry. Sara didn't understand that there were dozens of smaller universities in her state that were affordable and would allow her to thrive as a big fish in a small pond. (Look at all these fish metaphors!) And no one close to Sara was able to present this as an option. She didn't know what she didn't know, and she paid the price.

So what happened to Sara? Well, after dropping out of college, she worked her way up through some nice office jobs. However, Sara was constantly passed over when promotions were available. Those promotions went to her coworkers who had a degree. Realizing she had hit a ceiling, she made the commitment to finish her degree. At twenty-four, Sara went back to school and graduated from Baylor University.

Everybody's happy! It's the magical story of achievement against all odds.

So, was college worth it to Sara? Right now as I sit in a hotel room in California, preparing to meet with a college provost, she's at home putting our two children, Moses and Esther, to bed and will stay up late helping manage a company based in Florida from her home office. She doesn't need to have her degree to do the work she is doing now. **Strike one against the degree.** While the kids are young, she prefers to stay home with them; a degree isn't required for this. **Strike two against the degree.** Her passion is volunteering in our community. For her, that means hosting foreign exchange students and leading a group that brings together Muslims, Jews, and Christians to combat the crazy stereotypes that are getting people beat up and yelled at in public these days. None of these community service activities require a degree. **Strike three against the degree.**

But using sports metaphors has to be the very lowest level of information synthesis in any sort of intellectual taxonomy, right there next to fish metaphors. Of course, the degree is worth it because lifelong learning matters. A degree provides absolute freedom and future life flexibility—it is the ultimate option. No one can ever take that degree away from Sara. She's the first in her family to ever earn a degree, and the very act of accomplishment for Sara is probably worth more than any job she would be able to acquire.

But ...

Would she have felt the same sense of accomplishment if she had figured out how to make it work at the local college where she started?

Yes ... but you don't know what you don't know. That's why we are writing this book.

Can you see that Sara's journey through college was haphazard and limited by her circumstances, instead of designed and executed with an end goal in mind?

Okay, hold onto that and let's dive into my part of the story.

Ben Goes to College

My path to college is the exact opposite of Sara's. All I ever wanted to do was go off to university. When I was in eighth grade, I went to visit a Yale student who was a friend of a friend of a friend's cousin. The fact that my parents sent me across the country to spend the weekend with a Yale student when I was twelve is a testament to how helpful they were in putting me on the path to achieve my dream of attending an Ivy League school. This Yale student took me to a Yale and Harvard football game, which profoundly rocked my world. From the talk of Plato in the car, to my first stop at a Dunkin' Donuts, to the game where we all rushed the field at the end. It was the first time I had ever set foot on a college campus. Being surrounded by all those giants who were so cool and so much older than me, reaffirmed my belief that I was created to do this one thing: attend an Ivy League university.

This hero-worship went so far that after the student from Yale mentioned that writing in all capital letters indicted a certain type of thinker—and there were a lot of those types of thinkers at Yale—I started writing everything in block capital letters. I seriously hoped it would rewire my brain to prepare *me* for Yale. I hung on this guy's every word, and it really changed the way I approached everything I did in school to ensure I would be an attractive applicant.

All I cared about through middle school and high school was making it to the biggest and best university that would accept me, and I applied to all of them. Everything I did in high school was related to how it would look on my college application. I branded myself to be the student on track for an Ivy League education.

I went on an international humanitarian trip where I was changed more than the people I helped. **Check!**

I secured a spot on the varsity football team as a sophomore. **Check!**

That varsity football team had to be the loosingest team in Texas football history—we won just a single game in the entire three years I played. But that was okay because now I could explain in my college essay what failure meant to me and how I experienced true pain through the very real struggle of being a bad athlete. **Check!**

I went to SAT tutors. I spent weeks crafting my application essays. And I applied to over *twenty* universities. Everything I did was in service to getting into the biggest-named, biggest-branded, most elite university. And then …

I got a mountain of rejection letters one Friday afternoon.

No, no, no, no, no! It was earth-shattering. Except for Sara refusing to marry me at fifteen, it was the most heartbreaking thing that ever happened to me. (That this was so traumatic just shows I've had the fortune to live a really great life.) I couldn't believe it. My parents were very supportive during this time, but I think they shared my disbelief—we had done everything right. I was smart enough, I was the quirky kid from Texas, and my whole brand was that I was going to be a hoot on all those elite Northeastern college campuses, bringing my own unique sense of intellectualism to bear. Did they even know what they were turning down?

Six weeks later I received another letter.

I'd been accepted into New York University! As disheartened as I had been by the rejections, I was thrilled by the acceptance. I got into a college within NYU I hadn't even heard of called Gallatin. Gallatin was going to allow me to create my own major, carefully curating exactly what courses and independent studies would create my very own individualized degree. It was like the school was built specifically for Ben Roberts, and I had not done any research on it at all. Someone at NYU read my application essay and said, "Oh, look at this quirky pastor's kid from Texas—he's definitely a Gallatin student."

All I had done for four years was research universities and how to crack the code for acceptance. But those hours upon hours of work weren't about *what school was right for me*. They were about what school carried the biggest brand, what I was going to be able to tell my friends, and how exalted I could become when that school brand rubbed off on me in the form of a degree.

I missed the whole point: the degree is just a tool to build the essential blocks of a life worth living, a life filled with deep meaning.

If you didn't know, NYU is expensive. Most of the friends I made there were kids who came from rich families—in fact, I think over half the class this year comes from either oil money or Wall Street money. No, that's ridiculous. However, my time did overlap with the Olsen twins' time, so there were at least some famous people who would come in and out at their leisure.

When I realized how much my family was sacrificing to put me through school, I did everything I could to get out in three years, and I did it. I took a lot of classes every semester, took summer school, worked on independent study classes, and found a professor who believed in me enough to help me get through the bureaucracy of it all and graduate at lighting speed. I also rented a 500-square-foot apartment and shared it with three other guys since it was so much cheaper than paying for a dorm room. It was tight, and I got a job that started at 4:00 a.m. unloading a truck in a warehouse down the street just so I could have the warm water in the shower when I woke up.

I had a blast, and I'm so proud of that degree and what it means. I'm glad that I will always be an NYU graduate, and it would be my great joy for my children to also attend NYU if that's the right school for them.

It sounds like another happy ending, right? Just wait.

I graduated, went out into the world to find a job, and started my career selling cars. I didn't want to sell cars, I wanted a first job as prestigious as my degree. I was told by many people that to land the most prestigious job, my time at NYU wasn't enough—I had to have an MBA. What? Hadn't I just made it? Graduated from an elite university with a Bachelor of Arts degree?

Apparently not. An MBA—an advanced business degree—was going to fill in the gaps of all the business lessons

I should have originally had as an undergraduate student while I was learning cross-cultural communication or the other philosophy-based courses I had chosen. Therefore, I took the same approach to finding an MBA program that I took in finding my undergraduate school. Like Sara, I learned the lesson that when you take college or career advice, it should be **from people who are where you want to be**. There are a lot of people who love you, but that doesn't mean they know how to achieve specifically what you want to achieve. So, be selective and thoughtful about whose advice you take to heart.

Dear reader, you know what? I found myself standing at graduation feeling completely adrift. I had my prestigious NYU degree, and now I had that precious MBA, but I had **no idea** what to do next.

Sara didn't know exactly how she was going to graduate, but all along she knew what it meant to have the degree. She understood the meaning of the degree, probably better than I did with all of my inarticulate dreams and musings.

We both could have done better to merge the imaginative with the practical when it came to our college experience. Can you see that in both our cases, we should have taken a wider view of college?

We were caught in the old story: college as the end, as the main character. We didn't know how to use college as a tool to write *our* story.

College in Context

In case you need more convincing, I have another visual aid for you.

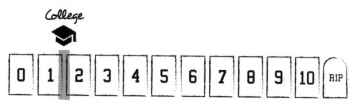

Your life, hacked into decades.

College doesn't get to be the main character because it's such a small part of your life. You see, you'll probably live around ninety years, and then you'll die like all the dead people who ever lived and then died. This is an important point we shouldn't gloss over too quickly: did you know that everyone who was ever born in the 1800s has one thing in common?

They all dead.

Anyhow, college will last four or six or eight years, and when you graduate you have a whole lot more life to live than you have already lived. College is important. It is the cap at the end of the childhood experience. It's the closest thing we have in America to a coming-of-age tradition, since it's the first time many of you will live away from the people who raised you. It's a time of great freedom and being able to test new things and ideas in ways you haven't had the freedom to do before.

To marginalize it and say it ain't no biggie is not right, but to deify it into something that's the end-all and be-all is shortsighted.

27

So, how do you think deeply about what comes after high school?

You can see from my story and Sara's story that we both got it wrong:[4]

Sara knew a degree was important to a future she wanted the freedom to create.

A degree was important to me because I wanted a brand that I thought would deliver me from my biggest fear: a life of mediocrity.

We were both missing our *why*. That's a critical step in learning to write *your* story. I'll show you how I found my *why*.

Finding My *Why*

Knowing my *why* allowed me to survive the first major crushing defeat of my life. When I graduated from NYU (before getting my MBA), my plan was to move to Vietnam and help Vietnamese high school students study for the SAT, coach them through their college applications, and then ensure they got into American universities. I was so excited. I spent my last year at school in a lot of meetings pitching different people on the idea. I met with the president of NYU to explain my idea and work out some sort of partnership where I could use NYU as my first partner institution for these soon-to-be college students. I worked hard on a business plan. I was packed and ready to move to Hanoi. I got to my final pitch meeting from

---

[4] Dr. Brown did everything right, so he doesn't get to write this chapter. No one wants to learn from raving success.

an investor who was going to fund the entire business. At the end of my presentation, he asked how many students came from Vietnam to study in America each year. I had no idea—none. This should have been the first red flag to myself that this Vietnam idea wasn't something I had spent enough time researching. I promised to get back to him.

When I did the research, I realized that in order for me to turn a profit, I would have to help every Vietnamese student who planned to come to America as a college student. That wasn't going to be possible. I was devastated.

This one small hiccup undermined the whole business plan! It was a bad business idea, and I abandoned it with one week to go before graduation. Maybe instead of giving up, I should have moved to Vietnam and tried to accomplish that goal another way. Maybe I didn't need $50,000; maybe I could have figured out how to make it work for $10,000 and built an empire. But I was too scared, and I wanted to do the responsible thing, so I gave up on the idea altogether.

All my hopes were in this business. What was I going to do now?

I moved home and got a job selling Hondas. This was a disappointment to me. But, let's be clear. This wasn't a disappointment because I, smart intellectual Ben Roberts was selling cars. It was a disappointment because my passion and skill set didn't have anything to do with selling cars. All work has dignity as long as it is carried out with integrity. As with many disappointments, I can look back and see how that first job out of college was a period of personal growth. During that time, I learned some pretty incredible skills about what it takes to sell, what it takes to build strategy, what it takes to ingratiate yourself to people who annoy you and are from different walks of life. At that dealership, I also met someone who really changed my outlook on life. His name is Thomas.

Thomas was also a salesman at the dealership, a couple years older than me, and he proved that hard work and persistence still matter. People instantly loved him; he was kind, but he was also able to convince anyone to do anything. I can't tell you how many times Thomas convinced a customer that leather seats were going to change their life. Thomas didn't have the same opportunities I was given, he didn't go to the wealthy high school across town, no one asked him where he was going to college, and he was forced to grow up faster and be far more responsible than most teenagers.

Before Thomas came to work at the Honda dealership, he was running a restaurant for a family. He was very successful at it—so much so that they opened several different sites across central Texas. They promised he would be able to take over the business. But, as often happens, that deal changed when the family's son reappeared unexpectedly after a long absence. There wasn't anything Thomas could do to secure his future prospects with the son back in the picture, and he wasn't going to work until 2:00 a.m. baking beans and smoking brisket without a path to joint ownership of the restaurant. Thomas has that unique and enviable spark that has always set him apart, regardless of his circumstances.

So he sold Hondas, and he did it better than me and everyone else at that dealership. He did better because he was willing to get to work at 7:00 a.m. when people were dropping their cars off to get an oil change and convince them they needed a new car, and he didn't leave until 10:00 p.m. so he could walk around the cars to catch the night owls who came to look when they didn't think anyone would be at the dealership. He did this six days a week for years. He was making more money than any of my friends with a college degree. Because of his hard work and determination, Thomas now leads a group at a luxury dealership in a major city where he is able to take care of his family and be an incredible father to his kids.

I share his story to show you there is opportunity out there if you don't go to college. That is fine, and it isn't a deal breaker for a successful life. But as I think about Thomas, I wonder how much easier it would have been for him if he'd had the same support I had growing up. My experience with Thomas helped me realize that all I wanted to do was find people like him and help them in whatever way I could. I didn't want to make them go to college; I wanted to make sure that opportunities exist for everyone.

That's how I found my *why*.

Knowing my *why*:

- got me through the work of selling cars when I knew it wasn't my dream.

- helped me survive the crushing defeat of losing my business idea.

- saw me through another two business failures that almost bankrupted me.

- helped me brave losing two jobs—one from a company I helped start and another at a company where I grew a significant department. Both times, my wife was six months pregnant—just to be safe, we aren't going to have any more kids.

None of those storms were terribly dramatic, but they stung all the same. Knowing my *why* helped me brave those storms.

The Five W's

What about you? What's your *why*? What are you trying to achieve with your life—what goal you are working toward between now and death?

That's heavy. But I'll let you off the hook a little. It might be nearly impossible for you to know your *why* at your age. People in their forties with lots of life experience and emotional maturity struggle to know their life's purpose. So it's okay if at half their age, you're just starting to figure out who you might become.

Even if you don't know for sure what you hope to do with your life beyond college, you can have an inkling. You might even feel really confident and have something written down. If you do, huzzah for you! My point is, in order to write your story, you need to start *thinking about your life beyond college.*

We're going to try to do this together throughout this book. Remember the Five W's we mentioned in the introduction? Those are the foundational elements we'll use to help you write your story. First, we are going to think about the **when**—the current state of higher education you're entering into. We'll explore **who** you are, what makes you tick, what makes you special—because you are special. Then, we are going to work through how you might articulate your **why**, your purpose. That will lead us to the **what**—your major. Then the **where**, the college or kinds of colleges you might like to go to, will become clearer based on this new self-knowledge.

See, when you give this decision about college just thirty minutes of your mental space, you can save yourself heartache and wasted time. Every decision you make there is loss-inherent. If you choose to go to Yale, you are choosing *not to go* to UT Austin. That's okay, but you need to understand why—and it has to be more than the fact that Yale's campus is so pretty.

I hope you see how this path can help you. When the storms of life hit, you'll be armed with self-knowledge, a useful college degree, and faith in your talents, passions, and aptitudes to see you through to whatever is coming next for you.

Why *Unbranded*?

This is why you are not a brand. You are a person with a story. You are not a company. I know personal branding is all the rage, but even those who are successful at selling themselves as a brand are careful to set boundaries and protect what is truly personal, like family and relationships. The lens through which we see the world radically changes our perception. Can you think bigger with me for just a second? Your story affects all the others around you too. And if you walk through this world seeing yourself as a brand, I shudder to think how millions of competing brands on the street will ever build a better world.

College is important. Trade school is important. The gap year is important. Going right into work is important. *IF* it's in line with your *why*. But if you're just walking through life thinking about what you'll do for a couple years after high school, your focus is shortsighted and flimsy.

With the rest of our time together in this book, Lee and I hope to convince you to ask questions of yourself. Take a journey of discovery into who you are, what you love, how you want to build a life for yourself in the next five, ten, or fifteen years, and what role college can play in that.

We hope you'll let us help you write *your* story.

2 Find Out WHEN

You remember from your English Lit class that every story has a setting. Think of the *when* like the setting of your story, and you'll see it working on two different levels: there is the *when* of your life now that you're old enough to be thinking about college, and there is the *when* of history. You have to think about both as you decide what comes next for you.

Johnny Tremain didn't go to college. Remember him? Did they make you read that book in school? It's about a young silversmith apprentice facing some pretty incredible challenges right before the Revolutionary War broke out in the colonies— before they became the United States.

It would have been foolish for Johnny to think about his future without also thinking about his unique place in history. He would have had quite a different story if he had ignored the Boston Tea Party and gone to the Boston Coffee Club instead. You don't know what the Boston Coffee Club is? Well, that's for good reason—our historical retelling can't possibly remember everything. Also, I made it up to prove a point.

Knowing the *when* of your place in history is critical as you think about what you want to achieve. What forces are

35

shaping our world right now that will help you decide how to plan out the next decade of your life?

It's also important to reflect on the unique *when* of your personal life. So, let's go from 50,000 feet to the personal—a global view of history to a personal view of you.

Coming of Age in America

Almost every culture in the world has a coming-of-age ceremony. Jewish kids go through a Bar Mitzvah and Bat Mitzvah to signal their adulthood. Children of the Sateré-Mawé tribe in Brazil wear gloves lined with the stingers of bullet ants to prove their toughness and readiness for adulthood. Rumspringa is an Amish rite of passage, a time when teens get to explore the world outside their close-knit community to ensure they are ready for a lifelong commitment to the Amish way of life. And then there is the quinceañera, the Latin American celebration for girls turning fifteen.

These traditions are important because they help instill a sense of past, present, and future. They help young adults understand their role in the larger community.

The closest thing to a coming-of-age ritual in the American tradition is a sweet sixteen, when some teens get their driver's license. If you're a kid in the suburbs, you were probably thrilled with the newfound freedoms that came with access to a car. But even this tradition is dying out as the need for a personal car wanes with all the rideshare services available. It's different from other cultures, too, in that it's more focused on *personal freedom* than recognizing your place in the wider community.

In reality, the move from living at home to going to college is the most obvious transition American students have from childhood to adulthood. So isn't it strange that this momentous event is the least contemplated by many of America's students?

Least contemplated? How can I make such a claim? Easy, I love hyperbole. Also, I have the research to back it up. Remember when I said I relied on others to help me decide what to do about my MBA and that I didn't exactly find people in roles I wanted to be in? That's pretty common. Only about 20% of students turn to experts in the field they want to pursue for advice.[5]

If you've spent a day at work with a professional in the career of your choice, or interviewed a family friend whose job interests you, or made a list of potential executives to quiz about the best schools for you based on industry expectations, give yourself a hand. You are way ahead of the curve.

But that's the problem—you're in the minority. High school students should not be relying only on their friends, family, and school counselors for advice about which college is best for them. That's the old story, where college is the main character.

---

[5] Lauren Camera, "Study: Students Rely on Least Reliable Source for Advice on College Majors," *U.S. News & World Report*, September 25, 2017, www.usnews.com/news/education-news/articles/2017-09-25/students-rely-on-least-reliable-source-for-advice-on-college-majors-friends-and-family?src=usn_tw.

We're talking about the new story now, right? The one where you're making empowered choices about how to cultivate the life you want way beyond school.

If you are, in fact, in that majority of students who haven't fully thought through how college should serve your career choice—or even what career path you'll choose—you shouldn't feel bad. This isn't a guilt trip. But you should pay attention because you're exactly the person this book is written for.

Who Can You Trust?

There was a tweet sent out when the ACLU awarded Colin Kaepernick with the "Courageous Advocate Award" for taking a stance that risked his job. One of the responders to the tweet said, "Well that makes one less college my children have to consider."

The joke here, of course, is that the ACLU is the American Civil Liberties Union (an organization that fights for the civil liberties of citizens), not an acronym for a university. So, we can safely assume this parent is giving pretty bad college advice by this public display. Receiving uninformed or outdated advice, even from a trusted adult, won't set you up for success.

Rewriting the story of how students go to college starts with rethinking where students turn for advice about which schools are best for them. This book is all about empowering you to take control of this decision, to write your own story. Your parents, teachers, counselors, and even friends might have some wisdom and opinions to share with you—which is great, and you should hear them out—but you are the one who needs to be making the final decision about university.

You are the one with the power in this story. Later in this book, you'll get to explore your passions, talents, and aptitudes. But before you get introspective, you need to understand the context in which you are graduating high school and moving out into the world.

So, who can you trust? It depends. If you're seeking advice about how to get into the medical field, talk to a medical professional. If you're thinking about law, talk to a lawyer. If you want to know what it's like to be a student at Texas A&M, for goodness' sake talk to a recent graduate. Go to the source first. Then, look for data.

As a society, we love stories. We love to hear about the student who applied to a hundred colleges and got the full ride to an Ivy League school, or the kid who spent five hours a night shooting free throws and became a college basketball star. That's fine; get inspired. However, if you are making decisions for your own life based on someone else's story, you need to be aware that, first, you are plagiarizing and, second, those results are not typical. If you want job data, go to the Bureau of Labor Statistics; if you want to know average debt of a student, read studies put out by the Institute for College Access & Success; if you want to know graduation rate, go to IPEDS.[6] These are tools available to you in taking control of your story. I know

---

[6] The Integrated Postsecondary Education Data System.

this all sounds foreign, but we have a page of resources in the back of the book where you can find a one-sentence explanation of these items and how to access them. You can also see this list on our website at www.unbrandedstudent.com/resources.

Current Challenges in Higher Education

We talked about the personal, now let's talk about the historical context in which you are entering college. There are three significant challenges you need to be aware of when making choices about college. We're telling you this because it probably doesn't come along with the advice you're getting from other people in your life. If you're going to take charge of this decision, you need to understand what you're getting yourself into and prepare to face these challenges.

Daunting Dropout Rates

The first thing you need to know is that a lot of students end up dropping out of school. According to a 2017 report published by National Student Clearinghouse, dropout rates range anywhere from 38% to 76% depending on where you're going to school! While dropout rates are lowest at four-year public and private nonprofit schools, they're shockingly high at other types of schools, like for-profit colleges and public community colleges.[7]

---

[7] NSC Research Center, "Signature 14 Completing College: A National View of Student Completion Rates—Fall 2011 Cohort," December 13, 2017, https://nscresearchcenter.org/signaturereport14/.

Knowing that dropout rates are so high should be an indication that graduating from college is not as easy as just showing up—it takes determination and effort and a little luck. Why luck? It's expensive, for one thing. And what we see with colleges around the nation is that students don't drop out because they want to but because they have to, whether it be over a financial issue, a parent needing help, a health problem, or any other number of reasons. It means you need to know exactly the financial commitment you are making from day one. It is far better to go to a school that is less expensive (even if you think it doesn't have the same reputation as an expensive school) if you have a clear plan to pay for that less-expensive school.

Student Loan Payments

Just because a student drops out doesn't mean he or she can magically forget about loans. Of students who take out loans and do not graduate, 24% default on those loans.[8]

This can get scary really fast. Defaulting on your loans has severe and long-term consequences; "it dramatically damages your credit, affecting your ability to purchase a car or put a down payment on a home."[9] And it still doesn't go away—your loan is turned over to a collections agency, adding collection fees on top of your growing unpaid balance. Finally,

[8] Judith Scott-Clayton, "The looming student loan default crisis is worse than we thought," Brookings, January 11, 2018, www.brookings.edu/research/the-looming-student-loan-default-crisis-is-worse-than-we-thought/.
[9] Shawn M. Carter, "Here's what happens if you default on your student loans—and how to get back on track," CNBC.com, October 9, 2017, www.cnbc.com/2017/10/09/what-happens-and-what-to-do-if-you-default-on-a-student-loan.html.

unlike most debt, college debt follows you forever—it stays with you even if you file bankruptcy. Talk about a ghost story.

Just imagine for a minute that you spend all this time, energy, and money to go to college only to drop out without a degree … but you still have to pay back the loans. Can you get a job that pays enough to support your lifestyle *and* your student loan payments?

Okay, you should take student loans seriously. I think we've proven that. But don't let student loans scare you. If you approach college intentionally and go out into the workforce, *you're going to be able to repay your loans.* Judging from the media, you would assume that everyone who goes to college is racking up at least $100,000 in debt to go to school. That isn't close to the truth. Sure, there are some students who have done this—many of them doctors—but the average student debt after college in 2015 was $30,100 per borrower,[10] which isn't so bad when you think about the lifelong earning potential with a degree.

Limited Earning Potential

A lot of the discussion around college is very focused on exactly how much money graduates make as soon as they shake the college president's hand and walk across the stage to receive their diploma. That's fine. You should be concerned about what job you get after college, but you also have to take

---

[10] Christine DiGangi, "The average student loan debt in every state," USAToday.com, April 28, 2017, www.usatoday.com/story/money/personalfinance/2017/04/28/average-student-loan-debt-every-state/100893668/.

the long-term view. You have to think of earning potential over your lifetime when you get that degree. In addition, these effects are additive because in recent years marriage patterns have shifted so that individuals with college degrees are more likely to marry, and when they do, they often marry partners who have college degrees. On average, here's what you can expect to make in a lifetime based on your level of education:

- High school diploma: $1.2 million
- Bachelor's degree: $2.1 million
- Master's degree: $2.5 million
- Doctorate degree: $3.4 million
- Professional degree (Law, Medicine, Pharmacy, or Dentistry for example): $4.4 million[11]

Since the above is so abstract, I have re-created the lifetime earnings for the different educational levels in the chart below using boats earned as the metric instead of dollars. Each boat is worth $500,000 of earnings.

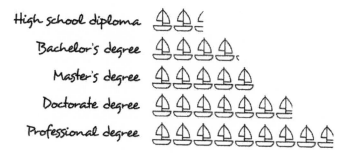

[11] Robert Longley, "Lifetime Earnings Soar with Education," ThoughtCo., June 4, 2017, www.thoughtco.com/lifetime-earnings-soar-with-education-3321730.

Those numbers might look big to you now, but you
: to break it down by month and factor in bills and living
expenses. What kind of life do you dream of? What do you
imagine for your future? Money isn't everything, but it *is* a tool
to help create the life you want. Can you have the life you
dream of without a college degree?

Is College Right for You?

Maybe your answer is yes. Some of you reading this
book might have doubts that college is for you. You don't have
to go to college. We didn't write this book to try and convince
every student to go to university; it isn't for everybody. There
are trades that don't require a college degree, and these are
extremely necessary for any functioning society.

**We are firm believers in the sanctity and dignity of
all work.**

But *not going* to college is just as weighty a decision as
going to college and should be made with knowledge and
understanding—not based on faulty data, assumptions or
anecdotes. Once you decide not to go to college, your chances
of getting a degree later drop significantly.[12] So this path might
be even more of a commitment than at least getting a degree.

Finally, there seems to be a perception among some of
the students we talk to that they don't deserve to go to college.
They believe that because of where they came from—whether

---

[12] "Dropping Out, Again: Why So Many College Students Never Graduate," NBCNews.com,
November 18, 2014, http://www.nbcnews.com/news/education/dropping-out-again-why-so-
many-college-students-never-graduate-n246956

that means economic class or parents who didn't go to college—there won't be a place for them once they arrive on campus. This is not true. Don't tell yourself this lie. *There is no such thing as a traditional college student anymore.* If you want to go to college, you deserve to go to college. It might be a bigger challenge for some than for others, whether financially or academically, but the point of this book is to help you find a place where you will succeed. We want to help you identify that place.

What Does This Mean for You?

The point is this: every path you take after high school is an important decision, one you should think about seriously. Can you see now that to face these challenges you have to be more intentional about your approach to college?

The old story is producing many unprepared, unhappy young professionals who regret the role college played in their story. A Gallup survey found that many students who would go back and change their college experience reported "having made decisions without comprehensive information, such as an understanding of employment opportunities, earning potential or the implications of long-term student debt."[13]

We can't save you from every eventuality or promise you a surefire path to success. What we can do is make you aware of the realities on the ground, so you can understand that

---

[13] Paul Fain, "Second Thoughts About Higher Education Decisions," Inside Higher Ed, June 1, 2017, www.insidehighered.com/news/2017/06/01/survey-finds-regrets-among-most-former-college-students-belief-quality-their.

choosing the right school has far-reaching consequences. We can give you a better shot at avoiding regret about your college years.

And this is about more than just going to college. There are a lot of other paths available to you. You can take a year abroad, if you can afford it. You could go into the military, vocational school, or straight out into the workforce. You could join a friend's business, or start your own. You can work your way up in a job that you started in high school.

What we want to do is create a paradigm for you to think deeply about how to use college as a means to an end to attain the life you are seeking post-graduation.

Our Two Cents

Speaking of giving advice … Lee and I are actually in a position to give advice because of our careers in higher education. We have seen students spending time, money, and energy without thinking about what it will accomplish for their future. Or students who go the other way and try so hard to be what their dream school wants them to be that they lose themselves along the way.

We called this book *Unbranded* because that's what we want for you—you special student, you.

We want you to be your own person, in charge of your own story.

Again, you are not a brand. Coca-Cola is a brand. Target is a brand. You are Grace. You are Jamal. You are a person. You are a special person uniquely created and endowed with inalienable rights, and you cede those rights little by little every time you force yourself into some prefabricated box in order to be a brand—for your family or your friends or your school of choice.

College is great! It'll be wonderful and fun and will make you hoot and holler. But it isn't a guarantee of anything. Figuring out how you can make the biggest difference with your unique set of gifts—and use college to accelerate those gifts—will help you more than any specific college.

We just want you to take some time and a few deep breaths; think about what is next for you. Put in the work to think about *who* you are, to find your *why*, to understand *what* major can best prepare you, and then decide *where* you can turn for the best education for you.

Where Do You Go from Here?

Now you know what's waiting for you after high school graduation; you know the *when*. If you're still with us, we're ready to help you explore the *who*. This is the fun part. Who are you? What are you passionate about? What makes up your unique personality, aptitudes, and interests? Let's find out.

3 Find Out WHO

It's a cliché that students set out for college to find themselves, but that's because it's true. It is hard to become fully independent and self-aware when you're bound by the rules and regulations of home and the authorities over you. Even if you stay at home during some of your college years, you need to start becoming more independent and prepare to launch into the world.

So, whatever path you take after high school—whether college, travel, or work—it's a process of finding yourself through those first important steps into adulthood. By taking some time to explore your passions, skills, and interests, you can craft a life mission to guide you post high school.

We love Maya Angelou. You need to read Maya Angelou. She wrote this incredible book called *I Know Why the Caged Bird Sings*. It tells of Angelou's life as a young black girl growing up in the American South. As you might imagine, she faced many difficult and painful moments in her young life. But she manages to write with so much wisdom, courage, and strength. Consider the last stanza of this poem:

The caged bird sings with a fearful trill,
of things unknown, but longed for still,

and his tune is heard on the distant hill,
for the caged bird sings of freedom.

—Maya Angelou, *I Know Why the Caged Bird Sings*[14]

I think about that title all the time; I'm getting chills writing about it. Obviously, this poem is about the desire to be free; a bird is the ultimate symbol of freedom. When it's caged, it cries out, yearning to stretch its wings. That caged bird might never have known life outside, but still it sings. Somehow it knows it doesn't belong behind bars. It knows it was made to fly.

If you can cultivate an understanding of who you are, of your deepest, truest self, you will find fulfillment no matter what life throws at you. The surest path to happiness is to find out what you love, what you're good at, and how you can use it to better the world.

Unbranded ... **Again**

That's why we're raging against this idea of you being a brand. Brands are the personification of the inanimate, the opposite of the uniqueness of an individual person. How do we create a sense of belonging for *things* that have no feeling and no soul? Why would you, as a person with inalienable rights, want to move backward and deny your innate humanity to become a brand?

Does that build community?

---

[14] "I Know Why the Caged Bird Sings Quotes," goodreads.com, accessed February 3, 2018, www.goodreads.com/work/quotes/1413589-i-know-why-the-caged-bird-sings.

Does that better the world?

You might say, well, it's a semantic tool to allow us to convey a complex message of how to communicate your personhood in a loud world. But if your goal is to create an effective megaphone through self-branding to increase your own power or wealth or fame for its own sake, you are always going to fail. You do you, and the notoriety will come.

In Maya's words: "Pursue the things you love doing, and then do them so well that people can't take their eyes off you."[15]

You are not a brand. Coca-Cola is a brand, Apple is a brand, your momma might be a brand—I don't know her, but she probably isn't because **people aren't brands**. And you, like your momma, are a person with a unique set of gifts. You develop these gifts into real talents. As you grow, you also learn where you are weak, and you do your best to keep these weaknesses from interfering with your strengths. The strengths you develop help you achieve your life's work, your mission, your *why*.

That's what makes you a unique person: the complex mix of your personality, your strengths, your passions, and your aptitudes. That's the *who* we're talking about in this chapter. We'll discuss personality, we'll discuss strengths, and we'll explore how to identify them. Then, we'll even share a small assessment we built called Building Blocks.

---

[15] "I Know Why the Caged Bird Sings Quotes," goodreads.com, accessed February 3, 2018, www.goodreads.com/work/quotes/1413589-i-know-why-the-caged-bird-sings.

Go to our website, www.unbrandedstudent.com/resources, to download *The Unbranded Brief: Student Personality Profile*. It's a tool to help you mark down the findings from these tests so you can monitor the way you grow and evolve over time. We take these tests once a year to understand a little more about ourselves but also to understand where our blind spots might be.

Personality

The American Psychological Association defines personality as "individual differences in characteristic patterns of thinking, feeling, and behaving."[16]

While every person is as unique as their fingerprint, personality can be quantified, identified, and studied. There is a whole discipline around this idea, and it can be a source of wisdom and self-knowledge if you take the time to study it. You might be wondering what this has to do with planning for your future. Well, psychologists say "if you're looking to see if you'll do well at a job, you need to see if you have the personality that fits the job, not just the smarts to do the job."[17]

Even a simple thought experiment supports this idea. If you're terrified of public speaking, it's just incredibly unlikely that you should be a lecturer or politician. If you are an overly active person who can't sit still for long, you probably wouldn't enjoy accounting or data entry.

---

[16] "Personality," American Psychological Association, accessed March 4, 2018, www.apa.org/topics/personality/index.aspx.

[17] "Which traits predict job performance?" American Psychological Association, accessed February 15, 2018, www.apa.org/helpcenter/predict-job-performance.aspx.

Don't get yourself into a situation where you've chosen a job that isn't well suited to your personality. Arm yourself with understanding of your personality as a basic element of career planning.

Plus, it can be fun. There are many tests you can take to give you insight into the characteristics of your personality. Here are three well-known options to get you started.

Myers-Briggs

The Myers-Briggs Type Indicator is one of the most widely used personality tests. It's based on the theory that you can identify basic preferences and organize them into sixteen distinctive personality types.[18] Each type is designated by a four-letter code. Reading about your type can give you insight into your personality and why you think, act, and reason in the way you do.

Enneagram

The Enneagram is a system that describes and categorizes personality on a spectrum. Though it has nine main personality types, each type interacts with several others, unlike a system like Myers-Briggs.

Learning your Enneagram type can provide you with a wealth of insight into what motivates your behaviors, desires, and thought processes. It also provides wisdom about how to

---

[18] "MBTI® Basics," The Myers & Briggs Foundation, accessed February 15, 2018, www.myersbriggs.org/my-mbti-personality-type/mbti-basics/home.htm?bhcp=1.

improve weaknesses or negative tendencies associated with your personality type.

The Big Five

Finally, a less popular but more academically rigorous personality assessment out there is the Big Five. In this assessment, psychologists have attempted to narrow down a host of personality variables into the most salient elements. This resulted in the five variables of (1) Openness to new experience, (2) Conscientiousness, (3) Extraversion, (4) Agreeableness, and (5) Neuroticism.

Strengths

One of the first lessons you learn in elementary school is how special you are. Teachers will point to your unique fingerprint to prove there is no one like you. However, even in our highly individualistic and independent society, we are left to think there are "sexy" strengths that stand above other, less glamorous strengths. Do you ever find yourself trying to be good at something you're not just so you can impress other people? Have you ever watched someone doing this? It doesn't work out well. Success comes when you identify and use *your* specific collection of strengths.

Be proud of the things you are good at! This might be harder than you think, especially if you live in a home with siblings whose strengths seem more highly valued. The reality is, people make a difference when they find out what they're good at and develop those aspects of their character. It is when you maximize what you are wired for that you are free to be the best version of yourself. It is also important not to focus too much on your weaknesses; don't let them distract you or weigh you down. You want to examine your weaknesses and understand them, but only to the extent they help you maximize your strengths.

Marcus Buckingham and Donald O. Clifton have developed a tool called CliftonStrengths to help you do just that. CliftonStrengths, formerly StrengthsFinder, is a series of questions that help you discover your natural strengths, uncover your talents, and learn how to use this information to benefit your life.

Think about what your strengths are and how the combination of those unique strengths gives you a competitive edge. Finding your strengths will be critical as you begin to think about your mission, vision, and goals. A touchstone of this approach is to identify your weaknesses as well, so you don't waste time pursuing things you're not good at. It's an idea based on the wisdom of playing to your strengths.

To find links to the Myers-Briggs, the Enneagram, the Big Five, and the CliftonStrengths tools, flip to the Resources page at the back of the book or visit www.unbrandedstudent.com/resources.

Seven Building Blocks

Now that you've done the introspective work to discover your personality traits and strengths, we want to zoom out a little bit. How can you use this newfound insight to pave your path to college?

In this section, we'll discuss some common broad personality themes we developed. We call these the **Building Blocks**. There are seven of them:

1. The Creative
2. The Polymath
3. The Builder
4. The Analyst
5. The Philanthropist
6. The Teacher
7. The Healer

These blocks are broader groups that encompass several different personality types and strengths. This approach was not developed to organize and label you by generalized strengths or personality; these Building Blocks are meant to help you plan for a post-college life that's in line with the way you are wired. For that reason, we developed each of these Building Blocks to help you align your personality and strengths with college degrees that might be a good fit.

Why call them Building Blocks? Well, you choose one or two that most reflect you and combine them with your personality assessments; your mission is to understand where your passions intersect your aptitudes. Test or no test—and we do provide a test—you are going to read through these and think, *Wow that's me*! It's because we have an idealized view of ourselves, and even if we can't live up to that view all the time, deep down we know who we want to be.

I know that you're special and you can't be pigeonholed into one of the seven Building Blocks that we have provided below. That's okay. Humor us. Try to find yourself in at least one or two of these Building Blocks as a way to start exploring different fields of study and career paths that you're well suited to. Which of these resonate with you? Does one of the majors or industries call out to you above the others?

If you read them all and you're still struggling to find a good fit, look backward. What kinds of activities or studies did you enjoy most as a child? Which classes have been your favorites through high school? Try not to think about this through a social lens. We're not asking which classes you liked best because your friends were in there or you liked that the teacher let you watch movies every Friday. I mean, which studies really ignited wonder and awe and excitement in you?

It can be confusing and frustrating when this feels like a puzzle you're trying to solve without having all the pieces. So if you get stuck, try not to worry. If you're thinking about these issues and genuinely giving this a try, that's the most important thing.

To go along with this section, we have developed an assessment you can take to help identify what kind of work might excite you. We believe you will be more content after college if you can shape your life doing something connected to your *why*. Even if it isn't always wonderful or easy, your future profession will be fulfilling in the long run when it's connected to your passions. You can find the assessment at www.unbrandedstudent.com/student-quiz.

Finding Your Competitive Edge

We are asking you to do this work in discovering your Building Blocks because it's important that you leverage what makes you special in your college search. As a professor of Strategic Management, I (Lee) spend my days teaching MBA students about how CEOs make decisions that can lead to improved performance for their firms. One key concept we discuss is how an organization can use its resources. Firms have the responsibility to analyze what they do well and what makes them unique, and then capitalize on those things. If they can offer something valuable in the marketplace that is rare and difficult for other firms to imitate or substitute, the firm can create a competitive advantage for an extended period of time.

This process is similar to the approach we are asking you to take in regard to your college degree. Examine how you are wired, and align that with a college degree and, hopefully, a career that you can enjoy. (This still doesn't make you a brand.)

Notice in the example above, one underlying principle to a firm's success is that the uniqueness of the firm is valued in the marketplace. In this book, we will not give you some half-baked follow-your-passion advice, claiming that if you follow our plan, you will never have to work a day in your life. Some of you are passionate about things you will not be able to build a life around.

In *So Good They Can't Ignore You,* Cal Newport shows that passion alone is not enough to make you successful in work. In fact, he argues that the common adage to follow your passions is poor advice. After studying what it takes to have a job that you love, Cal finds that individuals *develop* passions as they get better and improve at *what they are doing.*

Passion can come from competence and excellence.

Let that sink in for a second.

Most books about finding a job and building a life you are passionate about are written for an adult business audience. Many of them discuss how to transform your current job into something you love, or how to transition into a new career. You are not deciding whether to quit your high-paying job to follow your dreams. You are about to enter a stage where you develop the human capital that will be valuable in the labor market. Why not think deeply about the type of work you will spend your life engaged in and how to use college as a tool to help you get there?

You can achieve the best of both worlds if you plan it right. You can work toward something that aligns with your *why,* and you can achieve the competency in that domain that can lead to passionate work.

Whether it's Angela Duckworth's contention that you need Grit to succeed, or K. Anders Ericsson's approach of racking up 10,000 hours of deliberate practice to get to the top, the idea is the same: If you are engaged in a college program, and later a job, that aligns with your personality, skills, and interests, you are more likely to keep working hard when the storms of life hit. Remember the pyramid from Chapter 1?

You might actually avoid burnout and make it to 10,000 hours of deliberate practice if you build your pyramid with that solid foundation. This gives you a better chance of becoming great at what you do because you will be engaged in something you believe in, something you chose intentionally.

Vocation versus Avocation

One final thought before we get to the Building Blocks. When you're planning for your future, you need to think deeply about the dynamic between vocation (job) and avocation (hobby). You might love sports, but what are the odds you're going to go pro? You spend all your free time playing video games, but do you have the skills of a coder to one day make those video games? You're an amazing artist, but can you support a family on selling canvases?

This is where idealism meets reality. You have to decide if your primary interests are better suited to a vocation or avocation. For each of the fields mentioned in the previous paragraph, there are jobs with steadier income and wider opportunities that would still allow you to be part of the industry you love. Here are just a few examples:

- ~~Pro athlete~~ → Sports medicine, coaching, sports writing
- ~~Pro gamer~~ → Video game design or graphic arts
- ~~Artist~~ → Art teacher, designer, art director

Did we say not to follow your passions? No! You can be anything you want to be. If you're destined to be a famous artist whose work will be hung in the Louvre, then we believe in you! However, you can be smart about making the decisions post-college to help deal with high-risk, high-reward scenarios like going all in on an acting career. The above examples show how you can still be close to the action if you're unable to make your hobby your career.

If you need convincing from the real world, let's talk about the wildly successful company Warby Parker. Adam Grant, brilliant professor and author of *Originals: How Non-Conformists Change the World*, tells the story of Warby Parker. You might know the company for the way they've revolutionized the eyewear industry by providing affordable glasses that can be purchased online. It doesn't seem like a big deal now, but when they launched, people didn't think anyone would buy glasses online without being able to try them on first. The founders were actually in Grant's class at Wharton, and they asked Grant to invest in their idea. But after learning that the founders were going into internships or focusing on other activities rather than working exclusively on Warby Parker, Grant decided they weren't passionate enough by his standards. Grant gave them the advice he thought entrepreneurs needed. He told them that

"If they truly believed in Warby Parker, they should drop out to focus every waking hour on making it happen."[19] The founders response was great:

> We want to hedge our bets ... We're not sure if it's a good idea and we have no clue whether it will succeed, so we've been working on it in our spare time during the school year. We were four friends before we started, and we made a commitment that dealing with each other fairly was more important than success.[20]

Obviously, these founders knew what they were talking about. They wanted to test the waters before making decisions that would be hard to recover from should the business venture fail. So, should you be passionate about your ideas and dreams? You bet! But there are always strategies to get what you want if you are willing to be methodical and patient.

Most of you will find that your high school hobbies become leisure activities in your adult life. The Building Blocks in the next section are more about your skills, talents, and abilities than they are about your hobbies. So, yes, take your interests into account when reading the Building Blocks. But the most important question you should ask is: Can I make a living doing this? If the answer is no, that particular activity needs to be an avocation and not a vocation.

[19] Adam Grant, *Originals: How Non-Conformists Move the World* (New York: Penguin Random House, 2016), 15.
[20] Grant, 15.

Now that we have qualified everything so you're thinking holistically about who you are, what makes you special, let's talk about those Building Blocks.

How to Use the Building Blocks

We have developed our Building Blocks assessment to help you begin to identify which college major might be a good fit for you. By thinking deeply about your major now, we hope to set you up for success over the next four years and beyond. For the last eight years, I have taught the Capstone Business Strategy course to graduating business students. Every semester when I go around the room asking my students to tell me their post-graduation plans, I *always* have a handful of students who don't plan to use their business degree at all! These students have decided to teach or go back to graduate school for a degree in a completely unrelated discipline, or do something else entirely.

And you know what? They'll be fine. I'm happy they're making that decision now rather than ten or fifteen years from now when their freedom is limited by their responsibilities and relationships.

But these students would have been better off thinking through life after college **before** the last semester of their undergraduate degree. This is what happens when college becomes the final goal rather than a tool students use to achieve the life they want. From the time these students were little, they were told that the goal was to achieve the college degree, and now that they're at the end of that journey, they are finally taking a long look at what they will spend their life working on. Can you see that's a backward and shortsighted approach?

We are here to help you do that right now—*before* you spend four to six years on a degree that you might not use! So, how do the Building Blocks help you do this?

In the next section, we will explain what each individual block looks like in a person, a few examples of well-known people who display characteristics of that block, and college majors that fit well with that Building Block. We encourage you to read each Building Block before you take the assessment, which can be found at www.unbrandedstudent.com/student-quiz.

You'll also read about potential advantages of each block and common pitfalls that we see people fall into. These blocks are by no means comprehensive—they don't cover every major and every job out there. But they should give you a head start and help you come up with a list of potential areas for further study.

Think deeply about which two or three Building Blocks excite you and seem most relevant to your life. How are you uniquely wired? What value can your uniqueness add to your choice of college major and future career? We cannot answer all of these questions for you. These Building Blocks are not an all-encompassing personality test. You will have to do the hard work of analyzing yourself and your options, but we hope that by providing the Building Blocks, we can give you a framework within which you can make wise decisions about your college choices and your future career.

We freely admit there may be some personality bents and Building Blocks that align with trade work or other types of jobs that do not require a college degree. Again, we applaud you and encourage you if that's where you find yourself.

For those of you who do plan to go to college, we want to help you use college to its fullest potential. It is a huge investment of time, money, and energy, so use it wisely.

Now, finally, on to the Building Blocks!

THE CREATIVE

Are you the creative type? Many people love to create and engage in an artistic domain. If that's you, a key to crafting a successful career is to ask whether art is a hobby or a career for you. A life lived primarily as a creator requires the discipline and patience to create *every day* and develop routines to ensure productivity.

Stephen King, for example, writes almost every day of the year. In his memoir, _On Writing_, King claims to take only Christmas Day off, but then he confesses that he actually will write on Christmas, he just doesn't admit that to anyone. While there are examples of artists who create well with little effort or organization, it's extremely rare. In Mason Currey's book, _Daily Rituals_, he describes the habits of artists. A common and reoccurring theme is dedication to structured work routines. An artist, musician, or writer can't just wait for the muse to strike; like any other professional, he or she puts in work time every day.

Jane Austen, author of _Pride and Prejudice_ and many other works, was a true Creative. In a time when it was countercultural for a woman to make a living in publishing, she devoted her life to the craft of writing. Austen would sit down to write every day after breakfast as her mother and sister sat sewing nearby. When visitors came to the house, she would hide her papers and pick up sewing to conform to cultural norms and traditions. Despite these odd working arrangements, she was incredibly productive; she created timeless works that are still adapted and readapted for new audiences to this day.

Some of you might be excited by this idea of a daily creative routine, but you have heard countless critics insist artists don't make serious money and you should just get a STEM or business degree, and work in jobs that you hate until you retire. That is not the approach we are taking here. On the other hand, just because you like to draw doesn't mean you need to get an art degree. There are a variety of ways creative people have used college to successfully land themselves in a job they enjoy.

The great thing about being a creative person is this doesn't have to be your primary Building Block. Your identity as a Creative can help you across multiple blocks. Individuals who are successful across a variety of domains have been aided by their creative bents. For example, Steve Jobs was fascinated with calligraphy long before he ever created a computer, which led to a strong desire for computer font to be beautiful on the screen. He was also obsessed with the aesthetics of the products he sold, down to the inside of the device that no one would ever see. Let stories like this encourage and inspire you to think about the possibilities in your own life and career path.

You cannot afford to ignore the economic landscape when choosing your college degree. *Remember, college is a tool to help you achieve the life you want.* Very few individuals in your age cohort will be able to get a literature degree and spend their entire lives writing novel after novel. For this reason, Creatives—more so than some of the other Building Blocks—need to be thoughtful in their approach to college. Think deeply about what it is you want to do.

Do you want to write every day for a living? It might be a better plan to obtain a degree in business or psychology while taking composition courses with your free electives. You can then graduate and find journalism jobs covering your area of expertise.

Or maybe you are analytical and can handle a difficult STEM degree, but you don't love those things. Maybe you obtain the marketable degree, but in your free time you write, draw or act, while continuing to build your portfolio until you are able to capitalize on all of your hard work.

Some of you think those approaches are disgusting. You love art, and you do not want to clutter your life with nonessential pursuits that do not move your dream forward. If that is the case, it might be helpful to at least minor in business or entrepreneurship. Learn to market yourself and your art. With the rise of online marketplaces, and with the proper care and hard work, you might be able to develop a market for your goods and live a life focused on your art.

In his book _Real Artists Don't Starve_, Jeff Goins discusses the myth that all true artists must sacrifice any pursuit of wealth or comfort in order to succeed. The starving artist stereotype is a myth. An artistic life does not have to be one of suffering and lack, and starting out with that expectation is not helpful. Examine your life, your skills, and your bents, and think through a plan that will allow you to succeed as a Creative.

College Degrees for The Creative Building Block

Acting	Jazz
Advertising	Journalism
Art History	Marketing
Dance	Music Studies
Design	Theatre
English	Dance
Interior Design	

THE POLYMATH

A Polymath is someone with a wide range of knowledge, someone who knows a lot about many different subjects. Benjamin Franklin was a Polymath who made significant contributions in a broad array of disciplines. In addition to being a Founding Father of our nation, he was an inventor, scientist, author, diplomat, and hopeless romantic—among other things.

You might expect someone with as wide-ranging interests and expertise as Franklin to have a scattered and disorganized schedule, but that was not the case. Franklin famously wrote in his autobiography about his highly structured daily routine. He was able to achieve all that he did, in part, because he was wise in the way he used his time.

Many people, having seen movies about a genius like Matt Damon's character from *Good Will Hunting*, assume that every real-life genius has an innate gift for the abstract or is a savant who does not need to try. Those people do exist, but in the aggregate, people who succeed as Polymaths are willing to put in the long hours of hard work year after year. Those hours add up.

Warren Buffett, one of the richest men in the world and famous CEO/investor of Berkshire Hathaway, was once asked how to become a great investor. He grabbed the stack of technical pages he was reading and said that to become a great investor, you should read five hundred pages like this every day. Over time, that investment in knowledge acquisition adds up.

Those who fall into the Polymath Building Block are excited by long days spent reading about how the world works; they have the desire to aggregate knowledge from a variety of sources to help them make decisions. Individuals with the Polymath bent love learning, and the learning isn't necessarily siloed into a particular domain but is usually varied and extensive. This broad nature of learning helps the Polymath understand how the world works in a variety of domains. This unique blend of disparate ideas can also lead to new connections and new knowledge that others do not see. And this Building Block can be applied in a variety of fields.

As a professor in a very multi-disciplinary subject, I find this Building Block resonates with me. In management, we borrow heavily from sociology, psychology, economics, and other disciplines. We aggregate the theoretical insights of others to help us find and create order in the world. I love that at least three days out of every week, I have complete autonomy of my time. I am able to read for both breadth and depth, and I am given the freedom to do so in whatever direction interests me, as long as it is helpful in some way to my teaching and writing.

71

Many individuals who have a Polymath Building Block are considered experts in their field, eventually. The downside to individuals seeking a Polymath's life is that it takes time. No one is born with innate understanding of a particular field or domain. These things are built up day after day through hard work. In my case, since business is an applied field, I spent more than five years working at a large financial institution managing a group of analysts and a variety of projects and processes, so I could have some credibility when I stood up to teach in front of a classroom of master's level business students. I completed my MBA during nights and on weekends. After that, I spent another four years in my doctoral program diving deep into the literature on business strategy and trying to learn all I could about my field.

This path was a ten-year commitment, and it wasn't easy. If I had started when I already had children and a lot of adult responsibilities, I would never have completed it. Jobs that rely on a Polymath Building Block have many benefits, but you need to be in it for the long haul. Think deeply about whether or not it is something you want to pursue. In addition, think of some skills or abilities you can exploit and jobs you can work while you gain the knowledge you need to be considered an expert. No one is going to pay you to be an expert in your field right out of school. I don't care what school it is or what major you obtain. You might have a valuable degree that is well compensated in the marketplace, but you won't be an expert just yet. If that's what you want to achieve, please take the time to craft a long-term plan focusing on what it is you want to accomplish, as well as a short-term plan to fund that pursuit.

Please note, when we use the term *Polymath*, it is a bent and not an accomplishment already achieved. When most people use the term, they are referring to the diversified accomplishments of an individual's life—think Leonardo da Vinci. We are using *Polymath* to highlight the type of life you are wired to live. Achievement is up to you. We believe that college can help you get there, but your achievements will be the next sixty years in the making.

College Degrees for The Polymath Building Block

American Studies

Ancient History

Anthropology

Asian Cultures and Languages

Biology

Classics

Geography

History

International Business

Management

Philosophy

Psychology

Sociology

Entrepreneurship

THE BUILDER

The Wright brothers are famous for creating the first man-operated flying machine. Most of us know that part of the story. If we didn't know much more, we would think they were individuals with a very high-risk tolerance who sought to change the world. While the Wright brothers eventually grew into men who wanted to change the world, that wasn't their initial goal.

The Wright brothers were Builders at heart. Before they ever began working on a flying machine, they owned and operated a bicycle shop that built and repaired bicycles. Anyone who has ever done serious bike riding knows that proper bicycle maintenance requires many incremental adjustments to ensure the bike fits well to the rider. You can imagine that over a hundred years ago the mechanical knowledge needed to maintain and repair a bicycle would have been extensive.

The Wright brothers mastered this approach of improvement by incremental adjustment and applied it to building their flying machine. They worked on it day after day, making small improvements as they went along. After years of hard work on the machine, they took it to Kitty Hawk to test-fly it. Even after achieving flight, they continued to make minor adjustments to the plane and practiced their ability to fly it. Only after they were comfortable with how the plane behaved in the air did they attempt to put a motor on it. The motor had to be built from scratch, so they worked closely with the manufacturer, because at the time, there were no motors designed specifically for the unique needs of the plane.

Another famous Builder is the inventor of the light bulb, Thomas Edison. In addition to that most famous invention, he also invented the phonograph and the motion picture camera. Edison had a working process similar to that of the Wright brothers. Many of his innovations were made possible by the development of his research laboratory, where he had many researchers working and trying new things. The innovations were credited to Edison, but they often relied on the direct involvement of a team working alongside him.

Edison could credit his successes to his methods and perseverance. Apart from the meticulous work he carried out in his lab, he was dedicated to experimenting and furthering his craft; he outworked and outpaced all other inventors of his time and is considered one of the greatest engineering minds in all of history. Let his story encourage you; don't be intimidated. If this is the type of work you enjoy doing, it is possible to do it well through systematic and focused hard work, the continued pursuit of your goal.

When you read about the Wright brothers, Edison, or other Builders, does it resonate with you? Does this type of work interest you? You might love to be world famous, to be remembered in history books for your great inventions, but that doesn't just happen. You cannot look at the end result and decide that is the outcome you want.

The question is, does the lifestyle of a Builder and innovator appeal to you? Do you enjoy building things, fixing things, or developing something new? If so, you may be a Builder. One thing to note here is that the skill set required to make it through most of the Builder-focused degrees is heavy on quantitative abilities. Be sure you're up to the task ahead of you in the studies required to do the work of a Builder. To get through a good engineering program or a similar degree, you'll need a relatively high proficiency with mathematics and certain scientific fields of study. If you are not in a position to get through those courses now, that's okay, but you have to understand what you will be up against and be willing to put in the work to improve your quantitative skills.

So, if you'd like to work as an engineer, computer scientist, architect, or some other technician with a high mathematics background but you don't feel you have the current math skills to complete it, commit to working on those skills. Study hard day after day and see what happens. Remember, thirty minutes of effort four or five days a week can go a long way, and it almost always outpaces setting aside large binge sessions on the weekend or whenever you have a block of time.

What we don't want to happen is for you to read this book, decide that you have always wanted to be an engineer, and just assume that it will work out. Understanding the task in front of you should not discourage you but rather encourage you to work hard each day to reach your goal. The positive side of all this is that if you can get out of college with a degree in this block, it will tend to be highly valued in the marketplace.

College Degrees for The Builder Building Block

    Aerospace Engineering

    Architectural Engineering

    Architecture

    Civil Engineering

    Entrepreneurship

THE ANALYST

Marie Curie was a pioneering scientist who conducted research on radioactivity. She was the first woman to win a Nobel Prize, the first person to win it twice, and the only person to win it in two different sciences. Her research was pioneering new discoveries, but it was also practical and helpful, as she developed mobile radiology units to provide x-ray services to units in the field during WWI. Curie is a classic example of someone perfectly suited to the Analyst Building Block.

People who fall into the Analyst archetype seem very similar to the Polymath type; the difference is that the Analyst is more likely to focus on a specific field and is more inclined to be hyperfocused in advancing their understanding of that field.

Another example of a well-known Analyst is Alan Turing. Turing is the English computer scientist immortalized by Benedict Cumberbatch's portrayal in the movie *The Imitation Game*. In his work at the Government Code and Cypher School, Turing played a critical part in breaking the German cipher, helping the Allies to decode captured messages. While it is impossible to know exactly how impactful Turing's accomplishment was, experts estimate that breaking the

German cipher saved two years of war and over 14 million lives.[21]

Turing displayed Analyst tendencies throughout his life, beginning at a young age even when his analytical mind went against the approach of his early schools, which focused on a broad classical education. In addition to his more famous work during the war, Turing was a world-class researcher and professor whose work on conceptual understanding of early computers is still referenced today. With the recent rise in artificial intelligence, Turing's early work in that area is receiving revived attention as well.

Are you the type of person who loves details, data, or math? If so, you might be an Analyst. Analysts are information addicts. If you discover a subject that interests you and then you proceed to learn as much as you can about it in intricate and exhaustive detail, you might have Analyst bents.

As with most of the Building Blocks we discuss, the Analyst is a broad category. Analysts can be found in the fields of math, science, business disciplines, and computer science, among others. If you lean in this direction, you will have the advantage of a passion that is currently well compensated in the marketplace.

Analysts are often confused with Polymaths, but there is a legitimate underlying difference between the two. While Polymaths are more generalists, seeking to understand the

[21] Jack Copeland, "Alan Turing: The codebreaker who saved 'millions of lives,'" BBC.com, June 19, 2012, www.bbc.com/news/technology-18419691.

world through a variety of lenses, the Analysts seek to improve the understanding of their specific domain. The Polymath is generally an expert, able to synthesize disparate information to better understand the world, but he or she is not as focused as the Analyst. Disciplines that require a more focused pursuit of knowledge and demand high levels of competency at the given task are more Analyst-driven.

While the Polymath might shed new light on our understanding by bringing a multi-theoretic approach, the Analyst will dive so deep into a particular domain that his or her contribution comes from pushing the boundaries of what is currently known in that field.

College Degrees for The Analyst Building Block

Accounting

Actuarial Science

Biomedical Engineering

Biophysics

Chemical Engineering

Chemistry

Computation

Computer Science

Economics

Electrical and Computer Engineering

Environmental Science (Geological Sciences)

Finance

Management Information Systems

Mathematics

Neuroscience

Physics

THE PHILANTHROPIST

Some of you have already decided you want to spend your life helping others. Note, we do not believe that the desire to help others is limited to those in helping vocations. If you're a successful businessperson, part of a fulfilling life is giving back. Regardless of your domain, there are ways to help those who are less fortunate.

That being said, some of you might feel a specific call on your life to fight injustice or help those who are hurting. You might be a future social worker or religious leader. If this is you, then your path to college is an obvious one. Most state and private agencies that hire social workers expect at minimum a bachelor's degree. Similarly, most religious leaders are expected to have some religious training—oftentimes at the master's level or higher. We encourage you to pursue those paths.

Mother Teresa lived on mission. She spent the majority of her life in India caring for "the hungry, the naked, the homeless, the crippled, the blind, the lepers, all those people who feel unwanted, unloved, uncared for throughout society, people that have become a burden to the society and are shunned by everyone."[22]

---

[22] Jessica Durando, "10 inspiring quotes by Mother Teresa," *USA Today*, August 26 2014,

Mother Teresa started by opening a hospice for people with leprosy; she longed to give them a place to die with dignity instead of shame. As time went on, she was able to open hospices, orphanages, and houses for lepers across India. Her life was driven by a mission; she did not live for status, money, or fame. Ironically, for this very reason, she gained more fame and status than most people will achieve in a lifetime. Again, it wasn't because she sought those things, but rather because she gave her life to a cause she believed in.

Martin Luther King Jr. played a critical role in the civil rights movement. As a spokesperson and leader, his use of nonviolent resistance and civil disobedience led to dramatic societal, regulatory, and governmental change. King did not just stumble into his position of authority as the face of the movement; his efforts resulted from years of hard work starting early in his career.

We hear about King's triumphs over injustice and prejudice, but he wasn't always successful. A year before his famous "I Have a Dream" speech, King led an unsuccessful campaign to end segregation in Georgia. Such setbacks and adversity would be enough to stop most people, but King was driven by his mission. Like Mother Teresa, he gained notoriety and status during his lifetime, and after his death.

The lives of Mother Teresa and Dr. King, among so many others, testify to the truth that by following your passions, living on mission, and opening to your most authentic self, you

www.usatoday.com/story/news/nation-now/2014/08/26/mother-teresa-quotes/14364401/.

can do great things in the world. Significant, world-shaping changes can start with the seed of a simple calling.

If you are mission-driven, we want to put you in a situation to succeed. The data on social and religious worker tenure shows that missional jobs are difficult to sustain over the long term. The problem in philanthropic fields is that lasting change only comes about over years, sometimes decades. Mother Teresa and Dr. King would not have a legacy if they had quit when things got hard. It is because of their perseverance through difficulty that we live in a changed world today; that's why we know their names.

Our goal so far has been to help students find their *why*. You have already done that. You understand that you're foregoing personal wealth for higher meaning. For you, it will be more important to plan *how* you will achieve your *why*. You might be able to do that using your secondary Building Blocks. Since social work and religious institutions do not typically pay well, think through ways you can support yourself on the side.

Maybe you could minor in business and begin a side hustle so you don't struggle to pay the bills; this might allow you to fully engage at work without worrying about a low salary. Are you a helper who also has some inclination toward the Builder block? Maybe you should develop skills in building or repairs as a small side business. This is just one example of many possibilities.

Regardless of your circumstances, we suggest you take the inverse approach we've outlined for most of our readers.

Their task is to find their *why* and then plan out how to get there. You already have your *why*, but you need to be strategic and practical in preparing a career foundation that can support the mission you feel called to.

College Degrees for The Philanthropist Building Block

      Families and Society

      Human Development and Family Sciences

      Religious Studies

      Social Work

      Youth and Community Studies

      Public Administration

THE TEACHER

Anne Sullivan contracted a serious eye disease at the age of five and became permanently blind without the ability to read or write. Her parents were unskilled immigrants who did not know how to read either. After hearing about the Perkins School for the Blind in Boston, she enrolled and studied until she graduated valedictorian at the age of twenty.

The summer after her graduation, she began working with a seven-year-old child named Helen Keller. The relationship between Sullivan and Keller lasted forty-nine years. Sullivan used a variety of teaching methods before landing on teaching Keller vocabulary based on her own interests. Keller's remarkable genius is something we can all recognize and appreciate, but we should also be quick to point out that Sullivan was the great Teacher who was able to bring out those talents. Anne Sullivan left a legacy that still inspires Teachers today, and her work with Helen Keller helped to change the perception of educating children with disabilities and special needs.

Aristotle, the Greek philosopher, was clearly a Polymath, but his life is also a great example of the power that Teachers can have on society and in the wider world. When

Aristotle was eighteen, he joined Plato's Academy and remained there until he was thirty-seven. During that time, under Plato's direction, he studied and wrote on a variety of subjects. After Plato died, Aristotle became the personal tutor of Alexander the Great until the age of sixteen. This heritage of teaching helped shape Western Civilization!

While you may never have the heritage of Plato and Aristotle, teaching could provide you the unique opportunity to make a difference in the lives of your students, and then your efforts scale as your students go out and impact the world. Talk to any high school teacher who has been teaching for more than ten years. Ask them about some of their past students. They will have stories of great successes and dramatic turnarounds; they'll be able to tell you about lives they have touched.

K. Anders Ericsson, the social scientist we mentioned earlier who studies expert performance and pioneered the research on deliberate practice, notes that one of the main components of expert performance is to find a mentor or coach. Without a Teacher to guide a student, mastery cannot be achieved. It is the Teacher who leads the student through deliberate practice. It is the Teacher who guides the student to appropriate methods of work. Without the Teacher, the student might work hard and put in lots of hours, but the efforts are inefficient because they aren't focused on the areas of needed improvement.

Many of you have wanted to teach from a young age, and you can easily align yourself with this Building Block. But maybe you will find a less-direct path to being a Teacher. Some of you have known for a long time that you're not cut out to compete at the highest levels of whatever extracurricular sport or activity you've enjoyed. Maybe you'd make a great coach. Sometimes, teaching or coaching is the next best option. It can be tough for a high school student to know whether or not they'll enjoy teaching, though. And teaching is the kind of job that takes commitment, passion, and many hours outside of work. You need to be sure you want this before you pursue a teaching-related degree.

So, it would be smart for you to shadow or interview a teacher before you decide you want to commit to that path. Even better would be an opportunity to try out teaching for yourself. Tutor a group of kids or volunteer at an academic summer camp. Or if you lean more toward coaching, try coaching a kids' team or giving private lessons. Even as a student, you can do this for a reduced rate or for free, as long as you have experience in the realm of whatever you're teaching.

If you love it, it's confirmation that this is something you might be wired to do. On the other hand, many of you will realize that, while you love the subject or sport, you are much less interested in teaching it than you thought. That's okay. It's better to waste a few seasons of your life figuring that out now than it is to invest years in a career that you won't enjoy.

Teaching is one of the most demanding careers out there; don't go into it if you don't love it.

In addition to learning whether or not you enjoy teaching, practice will help you improve your teaching skills. Teaching is both a calling *and* a craft. The desire to teach should be there, but you should also strive to improve. Remember that passion and joy can come from competence. If you seek to teach, do it as well as you can. This will increase your resolve and passion for your profession and lead to a more fulfilling career.

College Degrees for The Teacher Building Block

All-Level Generic Special Education

Applied Learning and Development

Athletic Training

Communication and Leadership

Communication Studies

Early Childhood to Grade 6 Generalist

Kinesiology and Health Education

Teaching

THE HEALER

Some people have a lifelong desire to heal hurting, injured, and suffering people. There is a clear path to employment for those with this bent, and the healthcare industry is broad enough to offer a variety of jobs within this domain that you can prepare for in college. The great thing about this field is that the path is straightforward and well defined. You can enter college with a plan, take the required courses, pass the licensing exams, and find a job in your domain.

Benjamin Rush, as you might remember from your US History course, is considered one of the founding fathers of the United States. As a civic leader in Philadelphia, Rush was an active politician and social reformer. He was in attendance at the Continental Congress and was a signer of the Declaration of Independence. While Rush was highly engaged in a variety of domains and causes, he was a physician by profession. His views had a dramatic impact on the medical profession as we know it today. He promoted clean environments to aid in public health. For military personnel, he emphasized the importance of personal hygiene. He also contributed to our current system of evidence-based practice.

In the yellow fever epidemic of 1793, while most of the healthy and able-bodied left Philadelphia for a time, Rush remained and was praised for his courage and work ethic. He was said to have treated over one hundred patients a day at the peak of the outbreak, working day and night before becoming ill himself. While he is remembered more for his contribution to our young nation, it is clear that he was driven by the desire to see sick people healed. He sacrificed his own convenience, comfort, and sometimes his own health and safety to come to the aid of those in need. His example is a great legacy for those who hope to build a life in the healing domain.

If this Building Block resonates with you, you need to think beyond the job. Many of these professions require erratic schedules and long hours. If you are going to be a nurse, doctor, or EMT, you will often have more days off during the week than in other jobs. You may have to work holidays. Your schedule will not be flexible, and time off with family might be hard to come by.

Self-care is also important to people who choose such a demanding career path. Medical professionals, along with teachers, have some of the highest burnout rates of any profession. You have to stay healthy and balanced to deal with the requirements on your time, energy, and emotions. Many people who fall into a healer Building Block have found that if they pursue secondary interests during their time off, their quality of life dramatically improves. Your outside interest could complement your work, or you could pursue a new hobby.

Whatever this is for you, the point is that you need to consider how you might foster a balanced life in this potentially high-stress profession.

Another important thing to consider is whether you can actually handle the work. It might sound great in theory to help people in medical need, but if your knees get weak at the sight of blood or if suffering affects you deeply, you might struggle to succeed in a medical profession. EMTs have an even more difficult time, as they are faced with stepping into some of the most traumatic events of people's lives.

It is difficult to know in advance if you have the stomach for this type of work, so you need to think through the path you are taking when you pursue this career. And, if possible, get some experience before you commit to the career path. As with teaching, you could benefit from learning about the realities of this work ahead of time. Shadow a doctor, interview an EMT, read and research all you can, and try to give your findings an objective look before you go down this road.

College Degrees for The Healer Building Block

Health Promotion

Pharmacy

Pre-Pharmacy

Nursing

Pre-Med

EMT Studies

Next Steps

We get it. Choosing which college to attend and which major to pursue is a big decision filled with uncertainty. Reading this book and following our guidance will not eliminate all of that fear. That being said, taking a strategic approach and using college as a tool to achieve the life you want is a far better plan than the one we see most students embrace.

A favorite pastime of elders is to rag on the younger generation as one where everyone gets a trophy. The irony is it's often the previous generation—the people who handed out the participation trophies—who are the most vocal against the practice. I don't know about you, but I never received a participation trophy after finishing fifth and immediately believed I was the best. Despite what the college coach whose speech goes viral every couple of months would like you to believe, participation trophies aren't that big of a deal. And guess what? You are special. Just not in the way you think.

Most of you will not be the best in your field. That's probably not news to you. Most of you aren't even the best in your high school at what you like to do.

Still, you are unique. Your uniqueness lies in your combination of skills, interests, and talents rather than your ability to excel in your narrow domain.

Even if you're not the greatest in a field, that won't stop you from having a successful and fulfilling career. If you decide that you need to be the best at one thing, you will have a lot of competition; and, in the end, only one person can be the best. A better strategy is to develop a unique combination of skills that become more difficult to replicate. That's what will set you apart.

Every semester, I teach MBA students who are working as managers and vice presidents, among other roles. When I ask them who they have difficulty hiring, it's often candidates who have a unique, difficult-to-replicate skill set.

They're looking for the student with clinical experience *and* technical chops, someone who can act as a liaison between the very smart technology team doing the coding and the people actually using the technology. They need an engineer who also has experience leading and managing groups of people.

These jobs are difficult to fill and are highly compensated. They are also much more attainable than most people think. If you can combine your strengths with skills in complementary areas, you will set yourself up for unique job opportunities with little competition.

We want you to identify the traits that set you apart. If you can find a *combination* of interests and skills that can be used in a unique way, you can develop an advantage in the marketplace. This isn't just talk. The marketplace values candidates with unique skill sets and niche knowledge bases. A boxer has to be able to do more than just hit hard; he also has to be quick on his feet. A journalist needs to do more than just write well; she has to be perceptive and intuitive enough to think of the right questions at the right time and ask them in such a way that she can get answers. A great doctor not only knows her specialty but can synthesize the lessons of many different disciplines to diagnose and identify the right care required. You might want to be a speaker, but if you don't have the patience to sit down and write a book to advertise your expertise, it's unlikely you'll get hired.

It's more about cultivating a unique and powerful combination of skills than being the best at any one thing.

By now you should have taken the individual Building Block assessment and identified your primary Building Block. It's time for the hard work to begin. Remember, you are a combination of traits, so use your Building Blocks results as a starting point. There are many different ways to craft your life, and college can be a tool to help. But before we dive into the ins and outs of which type of college you want to go to, let's try to determine what you would like to spend your life doing. One of the best ways to do that is to try different things. Here's the deal, though, you need to do this alone. *You need to figure out if you truly like doing something, or if you only think you like it because your friends are doing it.*

I played a lot of basketball in high school. Basketball is a great sport. I still enjoy it twice a year when I get the chance to play, but if I'm being honest with myself, I really didn't love basketball. I loved being with my friends. Luckily for me, it was obvious that basketball was not going to be in my future, and no one dared talk to me about shaping my college experience around playing basketball. I just wasn't that good.

96

The next best thing to happen to me was that all my friends went away to university while I stayed home and went to the local community college. I followed that up with a local regional university. I had no influence from friends in shaping my college education. I had to figure out what I actually enjoyed doing.

You have the opportunity right now as a high school student to figure these things out before college, but you have to be willing to ditch your friends every now and then and try some new things! Look over the Building Blocks. Think about why you landed where you did. Figure out what types of activities you might enjoy and try them! I don't know what this will look like for you. Maybe it means doing volunteer work, or taking up a new hobby, or even starting a part-time job. Just be brave enough to step out on your own and try something new.

So, what's next? Hold onto your list of Building Blocks and get ready to go deeper. It's time to find out *why* these particular blocks resonate with you. In some ways, this is the most important part. It's the soul, the heart, the energy that drives you; this is the mission that gives the whole thing meaning.

Don't forget to visit our website, www.unbrandedstudent.com/resources, and download *The Unbranded Brief: Student Personality Profile*. It's a great tool to list the results from your Myers-Briggs, Enneagram, Big Five, CliftonStrengths, and Building Blocks assessments. You'll be personality tested out for a while, but this tool will allow you to track your results throughout your life, so you can see how you grow and change as you experience new and exciting things.

4 Find Out WHY

If you haven't already created a LinkedIn profile to impress a college admissions counselor, you might find it's necessary when you officially enter the workforce. When you do, you'll see it's like the career equivalent of online dating. If you're looking for a job, researching a company, or trying to meet others in your field, it's great. But if you think people fake it on Instagram and Snapchat—or whatever app is culturally relevant during the time you read this—to portray their life in a more flattering light, you should see what some working professionals write about their jobs on LinkedIn. Just as a fun exercise, search "life coach" on LinkedIn to find some wildly inventive job summaries. I have paraphrased some of the most ridiculous to protect the people who I'm sure have the best of intentions:

1. I seek to stretch people to heights they have never reached by making them believe in their inner wisdom.

2. Through fostering synergistic cooperation among teams, I unleash the power of people to take their organization to new horizons.

3. I'm so addicted to success I can't stop being successful. Some addictions are harmful and cause

enormous problems; my addiction gets your company where it needs to be.

4. I'm a boss, but that's not the whole story—how could it be? I'm really a servant just trying to serve the ultimate boss, and that has always got to be the customer.

5. People say they find me a wonder to work with and a true inspiration. That might be true, but what I am more than anything is an explorer for success. Your company is the ship, and I'm the captain ready to strike gold in the oceans of possibility.

Do you think anyone truly believes they are "addicted to success"? Doubtful. And if your career goals are just for show, they're not serving you or anyone else in the long run.

This is why we want to help you focus and articulate your life mission. Genuine passion and ambition combined with valuable skills are what get you ahead. And you need to know your *why* or your mission so that your work life is sustainable and flexible enough to keep you going through decades in the workforce. We're going to use *mission* and *why* interchangeably. Don't get confused; they're the same thing.

Zoom Out

Our last chapter was a real close-up, examining your unique personality, aptitudes, and Building Blocks. So let's zoom out. Knowing your *why* isn't as much about the details as it is identifying the theme that knits all those details together.

The planning, the details, the intricacies of your college and career goals are important, but remember that the storms of life have a way of messing with all your best-laid plans. Knowing your *why* can carry you through even the toughest storms. It's knowing your *why* that will chart a new course for you if something goes wrong.

Why mission and not career? Because the world won't stay the same for forty years of your work life. Because *you* won't stay the same over the course of all those years. The world is evolving faster every year. Jobs aren't the same from one decade to the next. And your desires, goals, dreams, and needs will change with different stages of your life. No one career path or job can perfectly account for that amount of uncertainty.

But a *mission* can last those forty years. It can last a lifetime. And it can shift and change and evolve with every curve life throws you.

Remember my (Ben's) college story from Chapter 1? I wasn't thinking deeply about the rest of my life after college. This narrow thinking caused me to take one misstep after the next as I focused exclusively on how I could create myself into someone who would be accepted to the most prestigious schools. But when I discovered my mission, my *why*, I finally had a framework to think about my entire life journey—from the ups to the downs and everything in between. My mission showed me the driving force behind my passions and my work. And it has seen me through more than one job, through several moves across the country, and through the transition to fatherhood and community involvement.

Our editor, Paige, confirmed this was true in her story too. She finished her English degree with a teaching certificate, planning to teach high school English. But during her student teaching semester, she realized that—as much as she loved her students—her true passion was working with the books she was teaching in class. After interning as an editorial assistant, she took a job in corporate publishing. Paige saw that a career in teaching wasn't right for her and wouldn't serve her students. She recognized early on that her *why* wasn't teaching, it was empowering authors to publish their books. Her jobs have changed over the eleven years she's been doing this work, but her *why* has never faltered. It's helped her navigate an evolving job market, publishing industry, and family life.

Most adults in the workforce will confirm this idea, too, unless they're miserable and adrift. But find any adult who loves their job, and I bet they'll tell you a different version of this same story.

Man's Search for Meaning

This is why your approach to your future has to be about more than college, more than even what job comes after college. Fulfillment and meaning are not found in one college or one job. They play a part in achieving success, but they're not the end. It's the *mission* that fuels happiness through every season of your life into the long term.

Let me introduce you to someone who's going to rock your world. His name is Viktor Frankl.

If you haven't read Viktor Frankl's book *Man's Search for Meaning*, I'm going to be honest with you: I'm very happy you purchased our book, but you need to put this down and go buy that one first, and read it slowly. This book looks like the back of a cereal box when compared to Frankl's brilliance.

Frankl survived the Holocaust by knowing that his *why* allowed him to get through any *how*. For him, this was a lesson that stretched back to Nietzsche, and really to the beginning of time. It is wildly unlikely you will experience a Holocaust-level event in your lifetime. However, the same principle applies: if you can understand your *why*, you will get through any *how*. And believe me, the *how* after graduation can get bumpy.

There is no struggle so massive that you can't come out the other side if you understand your ultimate mission for life, your intrinsic meaning for being. Here's Frankl in his own words:

> As we said before, any attempt to restore a man's inner strength in the [concentration] camp had first to succeed in showing him some future goal. Nietzsche's words, "He who has a *why* to live for can bear with almost any *how*," could be the guiding motto for all psychotherapeutic and psychohygienic efforts regarding prisoners. Whenever there was an

opportunity for it, one had to give them a why—an aim—for their lives, in order to strengthen them to bear the terrible how of their existences. Woe to him who saw no more sense in his life, no aim, no purpose, and therefore no point in carrying on. He was soon lost. The typical reply with which such a man rejected all encouraging arguments was, "I have nothing to expect from life any more." What sort of answer can one give to that?

What was really needed was a fundamental change in our attitude toward life. We had to learn ourselves and, furthermore, we had to teach the despairing men, that *it did not really matter what we expected from life, but rather what life expected from us.* We needed to stop asking about the meaning of life, and instead to think of ourselves as those who were being questioned by life—daily and hourly. Our answer must consist, not in talk and meditation, but in right action and in right conduct. Life ultimately means taking the responsibility to find the right answer to its problems and to fulfill the task which it constantly sets for each individual.[23]

Couldn't have said it better myself. I hope you have Frankl's book in your hands by now. Your mission should be broad enough to allow you to evolve as a person but specific enough that you can accomplish something tangible during your lifetime.

You've heard of so many heroes through the years: Lincoln. Einstein. Eleanor Roosevelt. Martin Luther King, Jr. Mother Teresa. Jane Goodall. But you rarely hear about their lifelong struggles—the focus is more on their victories. Lincoln lost many of his first runs for public office. For years of his life, the public thought Einstein was daft. Mother Teresa suffered a crisis of faith. But we're only told the end of their stories, which makes the minutia of day-to-day failure and hardship difficult to believe.

I can tell you from my own experience that it's putting one foot in front of the other, guided by your *why*, that gets you where you want to go. That's the story for most of us. Some of you reading this were born on third base; you're way ahead of the rest of your class. If that's you, the best thing you can do is make good on that advantage.

I knew when I went off to New York University that my mission was to change the world. This is far too broad to ever be an actionable life mission, but I read one too many biographies of well-intentioned explorers, so I believed it could

---

[23] Viktor E. Frankl, *Man's Search for Meaning*, (Boston: Beacon Press, 2006).

be done. I understood what I wanted to do but not how to get it done.

When I was six years old, my mom would take us to the public swimming pool, and I would jump from the high dive over and over. I was convinced there was some Olympic coach in the crowd scouting for the next big talent. At the time, I didn't think I wasn't good enough. I mean, who wouldn't want the Cannonball King on their Olympic dive team? I just thought the mythical coach in the crowd hadn't seen my best performance.

Then I approached finding a job after college in much the same way.

When I graduated, I had this expectation—which I thought was realistic at the time—that someone would be there to call on me to join them in the work of changing the world. You know, something non-profity and servicey and with just the right amount of gravitas that my NYU degree deserved. It sounds ridiculous now, but I give my younger self some grace because you just don't know what you don't know.

Obviously, this plan blew up in a blistering fire, and I was forced to reckon with the reality of modern life. I scrambled to find a job and ended up selling Hondas at the dealership back in my hometown. I had just graduated from one of American's premier institutions of higher education in only three years, and the very next month I was walking up and down lines of cars for customers, trying to identify which Honda Accord was blue with a tan leather interior!

But you know what? This was the place I found my mission. I realized that my life was about helping people find opportunity. I focus and meditate on that word all the time: *opportunity*. How am I going to help others find opportunity today? For those who don't have the parents I have, those who don't have access to the resources I have, those who don't have the amazing kids I have, those who are thinking about college in a way that isn't best for their long-term success and fulfillment. That might be you. Get it? Everything I do is in service to my mission.

Helping others identify and maximize opportunity is where I find the most fulfillment and where I am most successful, and it has become my life's mission. This mission is broad enough that there are literally hundreds of jobs I can do that will fulfill the mission. That means if I love a job and it decides it doesn't love me back, I can work somewhere else and still be on mission, not lose my identity. Will it be sad? Sure. Will I have to start over from square one? Nope. Because at the core of everything, I am helping people identify and maximize opportunity.

So here is the paradox: You don't fully know your *why* until you've gone through some real struggles and challenges. Some of you have; some of you haven't. It's okay either way, but now you've identified your Building Blocks. That's a place to start. That's a step in the right direction. Now take the next step. Follow the signs. Listen to the experiences in life that resonate with you most. All these things are arrows pointing you toward your mission. You'll get there. All you have to do is the next right thing, and pay attention to life as you do.

Don't be overwhelmed.

Here's what I want you to come away with after reading this chapter: there is a line between using college as a vocational training ground and using it as a four- or six-year exploration that will allow you to do amazing and powerful things with your life.

If you reduce your future to picking a college based on a job you want when you're eighteen, you are setting yourself up for hardship. How can you possibly know exactly what you want to do for the next forty years? How can you possibly know what jobs will be available to you after you've spent four years to get your degree? And even if the job you want is available, how can you guarantee a massive recession won't put it out of your reach?

You can't. That's the short and honest answer.

But if you know your *why*, it can get you through any *how*. So broaden your focus and begin to think missionally. Trust that the small tasks or jobs post-graduation all build on each other. Take what you need from each experience and believe it is growing you into the person you need to be to accomplish your mission over the course of your life. That's how our heroes and role models became great. Not in a day, a week, a year. But over the course of a lifetime guided by their convictions, beliefs, and passions. Following their *why*. Driven by their mission.

Lofty? Yeah. But this is your chance to chart a course into your future. Don't miss the chance to create a life of following your passions. A life you're proud to live.

TOMS: A Case Study

Let's get practical. Let's talk about Blake from TOMS Shoes. Now there's a guy whose story shows how following your *why* can make you wildly successful.

In case you don't know, TOMS became well known because of its business model, One for One®: for every item sold, a similar item is donated by the company to a person in need. But TOMS owner, Blake Mycoskie, didn't set out to develop the business or its inspiring model; he stumbled on the idea during a trip to Argentina in 2006. Blake saw firsthand the struggles faced by children growing up without shoes, and he had a business idea he thought might help. From that seed, TOMS was born. And what started as a model for selling shoes spilled over into new opportunities. Here's how the TOMS site describes it:

> Over the course of its first five years, TOMS was successful enough in providing shoes for children in need. But Blake, having recognized other vital needs during his travels around the world, realized that One for One® could be applied to more than shoes. He developed the idea for TOMS Eyewear in which for every pair of eyewear purchased, TOMS would help

give sight to a person in need. One for One®. In the fall of 2011, Blake released his first book, *Start Something That Matters*, offering his own amazing story of inspiration, and the power of incorporating giving in business. He references other companies and individuals who have been motivated and inspired to integrate philanthropy into their profession as well as their personal lives. The book became a *New York Times* best-seller. More importantly, it is Blake's hope that *Start Something That Matters* inspires others to turn their passion and dreams into a reality.[24]

What do you love? What are you passionate about? Can you let that drive you in whatever work you're doing? Can that mission help you—in Blake's words—start something that matters in the world?

If this seems a little too ambiguous for you, we want to help. We have an online course you can take that walks you through exercises to articulate your mission. Find it at www.unbrandedstudent.com/course.

For now, here's my favorite mission articulating activity: Writing your own obituary.

Write Your Obituary

This is morbid, but it's helpful. I want you to take ten minutes to think about attending your own funeral in the year _____. (As an estimate, do current year plus eighty years, but you only get to add seventy-eight years if you're still playing football after all the scientific studies that have been released regarding the impact of head trauma and what it means to the future quality of life).

Imagine everyone gathered for your funeral. You've lived a long life. Who is in that room? How have they been impacted by your words, your actions, and your work? Write down one paragraph of what you want to be said of you.

We all have family goals; we all have career ambitions; we all have dreams we want to achieve with our life. But you're not thinking about having the name of your college inscribed on your tombstone. I'm guessing in your obituary you didn't mention what college you went to because … life is more than college. That's the whole point of this book! We know from the data that you are likely to end up in college at some point in the coming years, even if you aren't dead set on enrolling right after graduation. It's natural that you're thinking and talking a lot about college, but it's possible to give it both too much weight and too little.

You give college too much weight by forgetting that it's only four to six years of a life that will span for the next eighty years. On the other hand, you give it too little weight if you don't consider that it's the first time living away from home, the first time you get to experience freedom in an American context, and it can be an essential opportunity to slingshot forward.

Now that I've really put on the pressure, let me just say, there is nothing you can screw up so bad in college that it can't be fixed while you're still in your early twenties. We want to help you think through how to make this decision so that your career goals fit within the larger tapestry of your lifelong hopes and dreams.

5 Find Out WHAT

The *what* is your major. We start with your major before selecting which college because the major is *major*. It is not uncommon to meet someone who went to college, got a degree, and never used it. But what does that really mean?

If you're going to college and not a technical school, the goals upon graduation are different. Technical schools are incredible because they focus on teaching a concrete skill—you go to welding school and you leave a welder. Welders are always needed, and they make great money right out of technical school. However, when you go to college and earn a Bachelor of Arts degree, you go hunt for a junior position at a firm that will teach you the specifics of their environment and the requisite tasks. The bachelor's degree, in some cases, can be extremely broad. Earning the degree signals to companies that you can do the work necessary, and they can train you on the specifics. Unlike the welder, the BA graduate starts work at Fidelity Investments as an HR specialist. She has to go through weeks of onboarding training to learn about the priorities and vision of the company, then she might have a few more weeks of one-on-one training to learn the daily responsibilities of the job. Do you get the picture?

The fact that the degree you earn isn't directly correlated to the first position you land doesn't undermine the degree. In fact, it shows the degree's value. Most employers have such respect for a college degree that they hire college grads even if their coursework doesn't exactly match the job requirements. The degree signals the candidate's ability to work hard, learn new skills, and finish what they start. However, imagine what more you can bring to the table if your college studies *are* aligned with your post-college work. How much more prepared will you be stepping into that role?

Now that you understand more about your aptitudes, personality, talents, and passions, you can use that self-discovery to lead the selection of a major. You aren't picking a job and working backward. You are picking a major and then building on top with the school, all while thinking about the eventual job.

The personality piece plays a role in this selection, but oftentimes we get bad advice when we think *only* of personality when choosing a job. A teacher might say a student who argues a lot is cut out to be a lawyer, but it isn't a person's argumentative nature that makes them a good lawyer, but rather someone who can spend hours on end reading case law to better understand how they can win their case. We boil the law down to what we see in the courtroom on a dramatic television series instead of talking about the true job responsibilities. The way we imagine a job is often connected to its outside appearance or stereotypes about the work that have nothing to do with the reality of the day-to-day work.

The work you did to figure out your personality might describe what kind of salesperson you will be and help you master that skill. But just because you're good at something doesn't mean you should pursue it while ignoring a burning passion for something else. Think about your teachers. You have had incredible teachers, some were extraverts, and some were introverts. Teaching isn't just for extroverts! Imagine if your introverted teacher said, "No, I'll never be a teacher. I'm too introverted." You can appreciate how both extremes of the introvert-extrovert spectrum can lead to excellence in the teaching profession. The same is true with every other job.

Why Major before College?

There are two main reasons why you should consider major before college. First, universities organize themselves in different ways. And if you're not aware of this organizational aspect, you can miss an opportunity right under your nose. This is confusing even for people who went to a college structured like this, so let's start from the beginning.

An Unforeseen Opportunity

Let's use an example of a made-up school—the University of Awesome. At the University of Awesome, there are four colleges: College of Business, College of Education, College of Healthcare Studies, College of Arts and Sciences.

At the University of Awesome (UA), the College of Business is well known, and it powers the brand of UA. Everyone knows of UA, but what they are really thinking about is UA's College of Business because their faculty members are the ones writing popular business books for non-academics, or being interviewed on television when the stock market takes a dive.

So, you decide you want an economics degree. At UA, economics is in the College of Business, and because UA's College of Business is world-renowned, it might be harder to get into than UA's College of Arts and Sciences. They might only let the highest-performing students into the College of Business, and your grades aren't quite there.

Here's the catch: DON'T cross UA off the list.

If you still believe UA is the right school for you and your SAT score is lower than you need it to be to get into UA's College of Business, then go ahead and apply to UA's College of Arts and Sciences. The College of Arts and Sciences is lesser known, and the requirements for entry are lower. You can spend a year or two in the College of Arts and Sciences and then transfer into the College of Business if you've proven you can handle the work and your grades are good.

One word of caution: If the goal is an economics degree from UA's College of Business, make sure you are being diligent about understanding exactly what classes you are taking during your time in the College of Arts and Sciences. You don't want to unnecessarily add a year to your time at UA because you weren't smart about picking your courses.

As you can see, at the University of Awesome, your choice of major can influence the college or university you choose. I know this seems convoluted—that's because it is! But my point is that knowing your major helps you make an intentional decision about what school is right for you. And part of that process is making sure you do the research to understand the structure of the school. To get this information, you might need to call the admissions office of the school you're evaluating. Ask about the organization of the school's colleges and which one your major falls under. Calling is a great way to understand the culture of the school and get information that might not be so easy to find on the university's website.

A Question of Finances

The second reason to pick your major before your school is cost. You deserve to go to college if you want to go. There are programs out there to help you pay for college if you don't have family to support you financially. However, we should still talk about cost as an important factor.

The reality is that most students don't leave with mountains of debt; the average college student in the US has about $30,000 in student loans to pay back after graduation.[25] So, don't let cost drive the decision, but consider it a factor as

---

[25] Christine DiGangi, "The average student loan debt in every state," *USA Today*, April 28, 2017, www.usatoday.com/story/money/personalfinance/2017/04/28/average-student-loan-debt-every-state/100893668/.

you think through the options. This means that if you're going to a school that costs $60,000 a year to become a teacher and no scholarships are available to you and no one is going to step in to pay cash for your tuition, it might make more sense to pick a cheaper school, so you don't struggle to repay your loans on a teacher's salary.

Imagine you did have someone willing to pay $60,000 a year for you to become a teacher. What if you chose, instead, to go to a school that cost $30,000 a year and you used that excess money to help start your life post-college. How much more comfortable would you be starting out in a field with low earning potential? It's okay to pick a field that has low earning potential. But that goes hand in hand with your decisions about your major and your school of choice.

The entrepreneur is like a teacher when it comes to taking cost into consideration. What if you are destined to be an entrepreneur? Does it make sense to go to a more expensive school when you could go somewhere less expensive and use the money you save toward your first venture? You need to think of cost as an investment. It is okay to spend more if you want a specific experience at a fancy liberal arts school, but just be aware of how that choice will impact your life during and after college.

The truth is, if you aren't going into a family business, you are going to have to hustle upon graduation for that first job whether you want to be a teacher or a Wall Street trader, so do it from a position of economic power. In the next chapter, we'll talk about how to put a college selection matrix together so that cost plays a factor—but not the deciding one.

Six Categories of College Majors

Now that you know why we're starting with your major, let's take a closer look at how majors are categorized. Below, you'll find six categories of majors offered by most universities. Based on what you learned about your skills, aptitudes, personality, and passions, which of these seems like the best fit for you? If you already have an idea of your major, which category does it fall in?

1. STEM
2. Business
3. Social Sciences
4. Arts/Liberal Arts/Humanities
5. Education
6. Health Professions

STEM

STEM denotes degrees in Science, Technology, Engineering, and Mathematics. These degrees are currently highly valued in the marketplace due to the undersupply of STEM graduates at American universities in the last decade. If you are a student who leans toward an Analyst or Builder tendency, you might find a home in the STEM category.

119

To succeed in a quality STEM program, you need to be aware of what is required. These degrees are highly time intensive. Two factors drive this intensity. The first is that it requires a heavy load of analytical coursework. There is no getting around the need for high-level mathematics in most STEM degrees. The second factor is more of a practical obstacle. Science classes require lots of lab time. Labs can take hours of face-to-face time each week, but they only provide small credit hours per semester. For this reason, science majors must spend more time on campus and in class than students in most other college majors. These constraints make it difficult for many students to finish a STEM program and can even dissuade some students from starting one.

We don't want to discourage you. But we think by giving you a realistic preview of what to expect, you can make a more informed decision about whether you have what it takes to thrive in a STEM program. If your analytical skills aren't where they need to be, you should spend time preparing now. You can do this through one-on-one tutoring, taking lectures online at places like Kahn Academy, reading textbooks, or completing workbooks in your subject of choice. Whatever you do, don't walk into a STEM program without preparing yourself; don't set yourself up to fail.

STEM degrees are challenging, and they have high dropout rates, but if you prepare yourself well in advance and you have the grit needed to get through, you will achieve one of the most valuable degrees in the current market environment.

Each year, various news outlets will release the top-paying entry-level jobs by degree, and engineering degrees continually dominate the top end of these lists.

Traditional jobs for STEM degrees:

- Engineer
- Lab scientist
- Teacher
- Computer and information technology specialist
- Business operations analyst
- Actuary
- Mathematician
- Data scientist/statistician
- Medical professional
- Environmental scientist and geoscientist

Business

I have a bachelor's, a master's, and a PhD in business, so I'm biased, but the business degree is a highly versatile degree that can open a broad range of occupational doors in a variety of industries. There is a ton of variability between different business majors as well. If you have Analyst Building Blocks, but you have no desire to pursue a STEM degree, a degree in economics or finance might be a good fit. On the other hand, if you show more Polymath tendencies, a general business or management degree makes more sense. Even Creatives with some Analyst tendencies can find a fit in the business school with marketing degrees.

For those students who don't want a degree in business, it can be helpful to minor in the subject or take free electives in the business school if possible. Understanding how the marketplace works and having a general idea of how to monetize a business or side hustle can be a practical use of free credit hours.

While business degrees are valuable in the marketplace and students place well, there are additional things you can do to improve your chances of obtaining the job you want. At this point in the book, you've identified the kind of life you want to live. Now, in addition to using your major to achieve that life, you can supplement your education with skills, experience, and extracurricular activities. A business degree combined with a host of relevant accomplishments and achievements can help your résumé stand out in more competitive job markets.

When I (Lee) graduated from school, I had three job offers in three completely different types of work. One offer was in a sales position, one in a small business, and one at a large bank. The business degree was valued at each of these institutions though the type of work varied. I took the job at the bank, which began as a straightforward analyst position. Soon after, I was promoted to managing a small team of analysts, and after a few years, I had multiple teams reporting to me either directly or through their managers. The skill sets required to succeed in these different roles were unique, but the general business curriculum helped to provide me the skills I needed to succeed. In addition, when I realized that my job wasn't connecting well with my mission in life, I was able to transition seamlessly into graduate school and academia. The combination and flexibility of skills you develop at a strong business school can provide value in a variety of industries. What you may lose by specializing, you gain in having a variety and combination of skills that the marketplace desires.

Traditional jobs for business degrees:

- Accountant
- Financial analyst
- Operations manager
- Economist
- Data scientist/statistician
- Human Resources manager
- Marketing associate
- Salesperson
- Product manager

Social Sciences

The social sciences are popular majors at most universities. In these degree programs, you will study either society or individuals within the society. These majors are also highly variable and include psychology, communications, political science, criminal justice, public administration, and anthropology, among others. Each domain will study a particular aspect of society or groups within society, or they will study them in a specific way. Social scientists use many of the statistical tools found in the natural sciences, but they change the unit of analysis to understand their particular domain better.

One key to succeeding with a social science major is to plan to excel on two fronts. First, you naturally want to learn as much as you can about the specific domain of your major. If you come out of school with a psychology degree, you want to have all of the knowledge that degree implies, but you don't want to stop there.

These degrees can provide a handful of transferable and valuable skills beyond the specific domain you are studying. For example, if you are a psychology major, you should expect to come out with a working knowledge of your field and an understanding of experimental design and statistics. Companies with a web presence are consistently engaging in A/B testing. Your skill set might come in handy here. If you major in anthropology, you might go to grad school and become a practicing anthropologist in an academic setting, but it's more likely that you will be hired by a firm. Luckily, with the huge

125

amount of data that firms are collecting, there is an increasing need for individuals to make sense of it, and using systematic observation to study human behavior can be a valuable skill in this economy.

These are just two of the many examples of how versatile a social sciences degree can be. The key here is to understand that the job market may or may not value your domain, but if you build skills and are willing to be flexible, the marketplace can put your skill set to use.

Traditional jobs for social sciences degrees:

- Psychologist
- Journalist
- Counselor
- Lawyer
- Human Resources manager
- Teacher
- Occupational therapist
- Public Relations specialist
- Sociologist

Arts/Liberal Arts/Humanities

Many people who give college advice suggest that students avoid degrees in this area and focus on more marketable coursework. That isn't going to be our advice. That would go against the entire premise of this book, which is that you should seek a career and a life based on your desires, bents, and skills. What we will suggest is that you have a plan and you do what it takes to make that plan achievable.

If your plan is to study the classics, and you only do that for the next four years with no thought to how it will help you land the career you want, you're making a mistake. If you want to spend your life reading deeply, you need to figure out how to find a job that allows you to do that. In today's economy, this is possible. Read deeply, and try writing about what you learn; start a podcast; or find some other way to monetize your interests. But you can't just read and expect to support yourself. Art, history, and philosophy are great majors, and they are needed in our current environment, but you will need to find some way to highlight their value.

Side note: You'll notice the idea of *monetizing your interests* is a recurring theme in this book. This just means finding a way to make money from something you enjoy doing in your free time. With the vast resources of the Internet at your fingertips, this is easier than ever, and there are mentors around every corner: a wealth of podcasts and blogs and books are dedicated to the subject. But if you just want a quick overview of the concept, check out the Forbes article "Six Tips for Turning Your Hobby into Your Job" for a place to start.

In addition to monetizing your work in the arts and humanities, you can use the skills you develop in your humanities courses in other domains. We're talking about *transferable skills.* In an environment where people are continually distracted by the buzz and pings of smartphones, there is value in being able to work and think deeply about complex tasks for long periods of time. In the book *Deep Work*, Cal Newport points out that concentration and attention are becoming rare and valuable skills. The intensive reading loads assigned to humanities students allow them to cultivate this concentration and attention. Also, many of the humanities degrees require a high level of proficiency in written communication, another highly valued skill in the marketplace today.

These are two of many skills common to arts and humanities degrees that transfer easily to the job market, but it's up to you to highlight these abilities in your job search. It's helpful to have something tangible to point to outside of classwork. Finding a minor that will complement your major can be one way to set yourself apart. Again, the approach you take will depend on the kind of life you have decided to pursue. Ensure that you're using your degree to achieve it.

Just remember what we said in Chapter 3 about vocation and avocation. Be sure you have realistic goals for how to make your work align with your passions, and if it can't, then find a way to pursue your passions as a hobby or side hustle.

Ben here. If you can't tell, this chapter was written by a college professor. I wanted to make a quick plug for the arts and humanities. Lee's right—they are versatile. My degree was a Bachelor of Arts. I wasn't gifted quantitatively, and my interests spanned everything. One week I wanted to learn about the civil rights movement, the next week I was on to trying to understand the best model for humanitarian work. *Is it better to partner with businesses or find funding? How can a business be run with the mission of a non-profit? Does that ever work?* My passions were broad, and the Building Block I most mirrored was the Creative. I was an extrovert, but I didn't know that sharing complex ideas would be fulfilling in my work life. This is why the arts gave me the broadest springboard for my future. It has brought me all this way to becoming a quasi-corporate person with entrepreneurial interests on the side. See, it's how all these things match together.

So if you feel liberal arts or humanities is the right path for you, don't neglect those transferable skills. Be intentional about cultivating a well-rounded skill set that can complement your BA degree.

Traditional jobs for arts/liberal arts/humanities degrees:

- Writer
- Graphic designer
- Artist
- Social worker
- Teacher
- Public Relations specialist
- Human Resources manager
- Salesperson

Education

One of the most straightforward paths from college to employment is an education major. Depending on the university, you will either major in education or you'll major in the subject you want to teach and minor in education to receive your teaching credentials, which are required for teachers in most states. Education majors are some of the few who, by and large, follow our main advice. Most of them decide they want to spend their life teaching, and they use college to obtain the degree that will allow them to do so.

One caution that we want to highlight for educators is the cost of college. This is not a book about financing your degree or one that harps on the high costs of a college education. Instead, we promote the use of college as a tool to achieve the life you would like to live. In the case of a teaching career, you need to keep a close eye on the costs of your education in order to comfortably live the life you want.

You have chosen to enter a field without top-end earning potential, and teacher salaries vary widely by state. A teaching career can be filled with meaning and virtue, and I am excited that you want to pursue this work, but understand that unless you are inherently wealthy or someone is paying for your education, it will be tough to live on an educator's salary with large student debt bills every month. Be mindful of your college spending so you can fully enjoy your post-college life doing what you love.

Traditional jobs for education degrees:

- Teacher
- Coach
- Professor
- Principal
- Academic advisor
- Personal tutor

Health Professions

Nurses, EMTs, doctors, physical therapists, and psychologists all fall under the umbrella of the health professions. Similar to teachers, many health professionals have naturally considered their post-college life more in-depth than the average college student. Degrees in the healthcare industry are in high demand across the country, and the path from college to employment is explicitly laid out.

A recent Glassdoor study examined post-college job choices, finding that nursing majors had the clearest career path; the overwhelming majority of nursing majors obtaining a job as a registered nurse, nurse practitioner, or nurse manager. The clarity of the health profession stands in sharp contrast to majors such as business, history, sociology, and others that have high variance for post-college jobs. Many students find it comforting to be on a career path with more certainty.

In talking with practicing nurses, doctors, and EMTs as we wrote this book, we found the most common piece of advice was that students need to make sure they understand what will be required of them. As a society, we need good people in these fields who will invest their lives in the health and safety of others, but students often enter the profession unprepared. College will provide you with the knowledge to complete the job at hand, but you should also consider your temperament. In many of these jobs, you will care for people living through the most traumatic experiences of their lives, and you need to be sure you can handle that.

Be sure you consider the demands and costs of a career in the health profession, so you can devote yourself fully to this path and enjoy the rewards of your meaningful work in healthcare.

Traditional jobs for health professions degrees:

- Doctor
- Nurse
- EMT
- Nurse practitioner
- Physician's assistant

College or Bust!

In some ways, choosing a major is the most challenging part of the process. You have to synthesize all the information about your talents, skills, and passions and hone in on one course of study. If you're coming into this process with no idea about what kind of work you want to do, that can feel really challenging. We hope that taking a broad view of these categories has helped you hone your focus at least one step further. From here you'll be armed to start looking at colleges with a firm foundation, charting a well-informed and intentional path to your future.

6 Find Out WHERE

Are your family and friends weighing in on where you should go to school? Sometimes the advice comes unsolicited and from all sides, and that can feel overwhelming. I'm sure they're just trying to help, but good intentions don't equal wise counsel.

At this point in your college search, you need facts and reliable data. In this chapter, we'll take a deep dive into the different types of universities you can choose from. Just don't forget that these are *guidelines*. Each school is unique and different.

Remember, the new story we are writing puts you at the center, not the school. You might be the first person in your family to go to college. If so, the whole process will be new for you and your family. My (Ben's) wife's advice to students in her situation is to move away for school. That forces you to learn how to live somewhere else and be part of another community. She felt that staying home and going to the regional public school was too similar to her high school experience; she couldn't really break away and learn to thrive in a new community. If you're worried about funding, remember there is financial aid out there. If you're afraid of the distance, don't forget about Skype. It's okay to be nervous, but making decisions based on fear is never going to lead to success.

On the other hand, for many of you, staying at home or close to home is a fine option. Some of you have responsibilities that don't allow you to take four years off; maybe you're expected to help support your family. You might be working and going to school at night. Or maybe you have healthy relationships with your family and you can take advantage of that by not paying housing the next four years. You might decide to defer the college decision and take a gap year or spend a year or two at a community college.

All of these approaches are fine. The data shows that more and more students are choosing universities close to their hometowns. *The key is to think it through.* Don't make your college decision lightly. Whether you decide to leave or to stay at home, you should take a methodological and thoughtful approach to your decision. Examine all the variables and make a choice that is right for you. In this chapter, we help you do that by educating you on the wide variety of college choices out there.

As we profile each type of school, you need to understand that these are general truths. The specific school you are targeting will be unique in some areas, so after you read this chapter and have gained a general understanding of the differences between types of universities, you'll need to research the specific schools you're considering to ensure they're actually a good fit for you.

The goal is to think deeply about the list of schools you might want to attend. You want to match the university to all the other aspects you've learned about yourself over the course of this book: your skills, talents, personality, passions, and your major. Remember, *these* are the key variables in your decision. Your goal over the next four years is to develop valuable skills that complement your strengths, personalities, and passions and prepare you to thrive in the job market. Your major is the catalyst that helps you build the skills and knowledge that will be valuable to future employers. That is the key.

Your choice of university should depend on all these factors, *not the other way around*. Students who choose their school first and then try to make it work are the ones who have the most trouble using their degree to achieve the career they want. In short, the school is a tool to help you live the life you want, but only <u>after</u> you have done the hard work of understanding who you are and what your situation is.

Is Public versus Private a Helpful Distinction?

When you ask most people about what different types of colleges are out there, they typically divide schools into public or private universities. This distinction isn't all that helpful. All this tells us is that the school either takes significant funding from the state or it doesn't. While this variable can have a huge impact on college price, which is a very important variable, the private or public distinction is otherwise not that helpful.

Many characteristics are attributed to private or public schools that *are not accurate*. To assume that an education gained at a private school is superior to that of a public school is not always true; quality of education varies highly by university. Even the common belief that private school education is more expensive than public school education is too generalized. This is true for most people, but depending on the combination of scholarship and financial aid package a student receives, the costs might be comparable. Here's the point: don't give up applying to a school just because you think it might be too expensive. You might be just the person they want to add to their population, and your desirability could create all kinds of incentives to entice you to attend their school.

One valid reason for choosing a private school over public school is to attend a school with a religious mission. Only private universities have this. Even in this case, you need to check your expectations before you dive in. Campus culture varies by university, but going to a private religious institution does not guarantee that you'll find unity in worldview or theology or whatever your rubric is. That said, your chances of finding like-minded students are higher in that environment than at a state school.

If you're a parent reading this and you want to protect your student from the outside world, I'm sorry to say that's nearly impossible—you're better off keeping your child at home. If an eighteen- to twenty-two-year-old wants to find a party, they can find it. This is true whether you're talking about a religious institution or not. If you don't believe me, Google it. As a professor, I can tell you there is one thing that you can achieve by sending your child to a private religious university, and that is faculty that generally have the same principles and beliefs you do. While this isn't always true, many of these schools require faculty to sign a code of ethics or a statement of faith. While it is difficult to enforce, it is a highly effective way of controlling who you allow to teach in college classrooms. I've found that many of my colleagues self-select out of the applicant pool when they realize that a school is serious about the faith or ethics of their professors if they don't fit. If this is important to you, I suggest you do some research on the schools you're targeting and see if they require their faculty to sign a statement of faith or code of religious ethics.

In summary, the private versus public school distinction can be informative, but it's just not the most helpful variable to consider. Many people cannot afford the private school experience. We are not writing a book on school finance, but we just want to acknowledge that *choosing an expensive education is only appropriate if you have a good reason to do so.* And the label of "private university" is not a good enough reason in and of itself. Truly examine the university in question and understand the decision you are making. In the next section, we'll discuss different types of colleges and universities. It's better to examine schools on these variables going forward.

Considering Universities by Type

The rest of this chapter is an examination of university by different type: community college, liberal arts college, regional four-year university, large state university, elite universities, and HBCUs. There's also a section written by a former student of an all-women's school in which she shares her experience.

There are thousands of ways to dissect and explain the different types of universities; for example, we didn't include a Hispanic Serving Institution, Alaskan Native or Native Hawaiian Institution, Tribal College and University, or anything about technical schools, and on and on. We didn't do that because this chapter serves as a primer. We want to give you a foundation on which to start your research.

When you're thinking about the different types of colleges available, two factors you should consider are *size* and *environment*. Big schools with 20,000 students are obviously different than small schools with 2,000 students. An urban campus is different from a rural campus. A school that serves a majority of commuters will feel different than a school where every student is required to live on campus their first year. As you get a high-level understanding of each of the school types we describe in the following pages, consider those factors to make sure you understand where a school falls on the spectrum.

The reality is, to get a real sense of the place and its environment, you have to visit the school; you have to go shake hands with current students; you have to walk the quad; you have to look at the dorms and sit in a classroom. I went to New York University for my undergraduate and then Baylor for my MBA. They are both private schools, but they provided radically different experiences, and I had no way of knowing that until I was there in person. So, once you narrow down your list of schools, make it a priority to visit the front-runners. I guarantee it will impact your decision.

Finally, when you're done reading through these different types of schools, go to www.unbrandedstudent.com/resources to find *The Unbranded College Search Matrix*. We created this helpful guide to evaluating schools, and it ignores all of the different school rankings. You need to pick the school that's best for *you*, and it might not be a school in the Top 20 List. You need to think of the metrics that are meaningful to you when picking a school, and having the data side by side on one piece of paper is extremely helpful.

Community College

By definition, a community college is "a two-year school that offers reasonably priced higher education as a pathway to a four-year degree."[26] Community colleges fill two primary needs to two very different types of students.

First, community colleges provide workforce training for a variety of skills, trades, and occupations through associate degrees and other certificate-based trainings. Community

---

[26] Brianna Burrows, "What is a Community College in the USA?" studyusa.com, accessed February 25, 2018, https://studyusa.com/en/a/1236/what-is-a-community-college-in-the-usa.

colleges can be an affordable and convenient way to learn a new trade or achieve certification needed to practice in your state. Second, students seeking credits to transfer to a four-year college or university in the future can use community college to their advantage. We will focus on the second set of students in this section.

Community college can be an extremely helpful and cost-effective way to knock out a significant chunk of college credit at an absurdly low cost. When I (Lee) went, community college was a fraction of the cost of the local four-year university, and since that time, the school has set up an agreement with the local high school to grant free tuition to all high school graduates! Community college can be an amazing deal for those who don't have the finances or can't move away to go to school.

The downside is, community college can also be a place people go and rack up a ton of college credit that isn't counted toward a four-year degree. I had a great experience with my local community college. It was ten minutes from the house I grew up in, and I spent my first fall, spring, and summer terms after high school taking as many classes as I could. At the end of my first year, I had over fifty college credits, and that year set the path for allowing me to finish my undergraduate degree in three years. Honestly, no one really cares where you spent your first year or two at school—no one at work, in your personal life, or on admissions committees for master's or PhD programs will bat an eye if they find out you started at a community college. This option can be a great tool, but you must use it wisely.

The reputation of a community college is that it's for high school graduates to land somewhere because they are unsure of what to do with their future—community college is a cheap place to figure it out. This is 100% not true. As you look at graduation rates, you will see community colleges have some of the lowest rates. This is because a lot of students transfer out, but also because if you don't know exactly what you're doing once you get out, and how you're using your time at the community college to achieve your goals, you are highly unlikely to succeed. The reality of a community college is opposite of the perception. To succeed at community college, you need to be much *more* focused and prepared. You'll be going to school with a lot of working adults with kids, high school grads with full-time jobs, and people in the workforce looking to perfect their skills. Community college can be fun, and there is good community at this type of school, but it is for serious students; you aren't going to get the handholding and care you will at other schools. Oftentimes, their size and complexity don't allow for the atmosphere that a liberal arts school is known for.

The strategy of taking classes at community college toward my four-year degree worked in my favor. I found the eventual degree I wanted first, and I made sure that every course I took went toward that degree program. At the time, I thought that was what everyone did. I didn't think anything I was doing was novel or special. Unfortunately, many students miss this opportunity![27] The students who are able to use community college as a tool are the ones who enter with a plan.

Also, please remember: the associate degree is not the end goal. I never achieved an associate degree because the school wanted me to take twelve credit hours of courses that wouldn't transfer. Never in my life have I regretted that decision. With few exceptions—like the trade and certificate jobs mentioned earlier—community college is best used as an inexpensive bridge between high school and your final college or university. But if you go the community college route, you need to have a long-term plan just as much as—if not more than—other students.

Here is an unrelated pro tip for those of you who are choosing to start at a community college: save your free electives for your final university. This can be helpful in several ways. First, your final university will likely have a wider range and more interesting set of classes to choose from to fulfill your elective requirements. Second, many schools don't count the GPA that you attained in classes that you transfer. If you find yourself in a situation where you need to increase your GPA, it's nice to have some free electives to do that with instead of only having the more difficult junior- and senior-level courses remaining in your discipline.

---

[27] Meredith Kolodner, "Why are graduation rates at community colleges so low?" The Hechinger Report, May 5, 2015, http://hechingerreport.org/new-book-addresses-low-community-college-graduation-rates/.

Liberal Arts College

The term *liberal arts college* is thrown around a lot. The definition will vary depending on who is defining the term, but these colleges usually focus on undergrad education in the arts and sciences. Liberal arts colleges often have a common curriculum that all students must take. This can be a small set of intensive primary classes or an entire two-year block of coursework that everyone takes together, but the goal is to provide a broad, general knowledge base that is both shared by students of the university and helpful to develop graduates with intellectual abilities to succeed after college. In short, the common curriculum serves as a unifying feature among students.

My (Lee's) wife attended a small liberal arts college that did not have a large two-year unified block of study but, rather, a few intensive classes that the school requires everyone to take. When she meets fellow alumni, it never fails that the conversation will at some point turn to their Western Civilization coursework (which they oddly all refer to as Civ). As someone who went to a large regional university, I do not understand this experience. I have more in common with a business major at a different university than I would an engineering or social work major who attended my alma mater. This fragmentation of the student experience isn't as strong in liberal arts colleges. The shared coursework gives students a unified sense of purpose and meaning, and these commonalities can make for a more positive and connected college experience.

Liberal arts colleges also typically do well at providing a broad and diversified educational experience. In larger universities, it is much easier to specialize. This has its advantages, but one disadvantage is that it's easier to get out of school with little to no exposure to some content. Since graduation, I have had to go back and read a great deal on philosophy, history, literature, and other subjects I feel like I missed out on as I raced through my undergraduate degree. I wouldn't have gotten away with that at a liberal arts college.

Another difference is that liberal arts colleges are generally more teaching-focused—meaning, the faculty are less concerned with doing original research.

Not all teaching institutions are created equal, so be sure to know how to judge the schools you are researching. The school might say they are teaching-focused, but sometimes to offset the less-rigorous faculty research expectations at these institutions, the teaching loads can be much higher than at larger, more research-intensive schools. Ask questions about what kind of course loads your professors will be teaching. If they are twice that of your nearby regional university, you might not be getting a more hands-on approach because the professors are too busy keeping up with their classes.

Liberal arts institutions are often lauded for their smaller class sizes and greater student–instructor interaction. If you are looking for a faculty member to help mentor you, or if you need a strong recommendation letter to achieve your post-college plans, then a liberal arts college might make sense for you.

Regional Four-Year University

Regional four-year universities might have the highest variance of any category of school. In more populated areas, these schools can have enrollments of 10,000 students or more, while less densely populated areas might only support a regional university of a few thousand. I have a great deal of experience with these types of institutions from both a student and faculty perspective. I have taught at large regional universities (40,000 students) as well as smaller schools (less than 3,000 students). After community college, I attended a large regional university for all my secondary education, including my bachelor's, master's, and doctoral work. For me, the key drivers of this decision were cost and location. I am lucky to live within driving distance of multiple regional four-year universities, so I had my pick. Not all areas are like this, but location is a large draw for most of these regional universities. The ability to stay relatively close to home is key for many students' situation.

Regional four-year universities are also highly competitive on cost. They fill a needed middle ground between the largely populated state institutions and smaller liberal arts colleges, in that they typically are large enough to offer a robust set of degrees and course offerings, but not so large that you become just another student going through the program. The wide variety in regional four-year universities leads to unique specializations and focuses that vary by school. Investigate the schools near you, talk to people in the workforce, and find out what the school is known for.

If you plan to start your career in your hometown, a good regional four-year university might have as strong a reputation as a large state university. The problem is that these reputations are not consistent everywhere you go. Your degree might be more valuable in the area where the university is well known. Most of these schools are not large enough to have a national reputation. Ten years into your career, it won't matter. Your work experience and the knowledge, skills, and abilities you bring to a company will earn you a good job, but to place well in your first post-college job, you might be more location-constrained if you are coming from a regional four-year university. For many people, this is ideal; but for some, this might steer you away from this option.

Large State University

Large state universities are some of the most well-known colleges in the United States. They are the largest schools that play each other in football on national television on Saturdays in the fall and whose jerseys are sold in sports stores across the nation. From an academic standpoint, these universities, due to their size, offer the most robust and varied classes, coursework, and degree plans of all the college options available. If you have a niche degree you would like to pursue, a large state university might be your only option.

150

In addition to course offerings and degree plans, one advantage that large state universities have is the built-in network. They do not have the small class sizes and the tight-knit community built around standard courses you will receive in a liberal arts college, but they make up for that in scale. They have so many graduates that when you earn a diploma, you are now in their club.

In my state, Texas A&M University is the best example of this phenomenon. I honestly don't get it from the outside looking in, but they are a club. You can spot an Aggie from a mile away. Oftentimes they are wearing the maroon school color and sporting the large class ring. I know people who have named their child Kyle after Kyle Field, the stadium in College Station where the Aggies play football. They have a shared language, shared hand motions they learn to mimic during football games, and a host of other shared traditions and experiences unique to the students of Texas A&M University. To those not part of the club, it can seem rather cultish, but there is no denying the fact that the system works. The built-in network available to graduates is highly valuable. Aggies hire Aggies. Love them or hate them, you can't deny there is value in graduating into such a strong college network.

If you want to attend a large state university, examine the industry you wish to work in and see if a school has a strong pipeline of former students in a ready-made network. If you expect to need a large, well-developed network to gain access to your industry of choice or to gain promotions throughout your career, a large state university might be the right place for you.

On the other hand, you will want to avoid a common mistake students make: being blinded by the cool factor. These schools are generally fine, but don't overvalue a school because of the football team. College sports change, and they can change rapidly. If you went to SMU in the eighties or, more recently, Penn State or Baylor because you wanted a lifetime of watching quality college football, you're going to be disappointed. Recent scandals have set those programs back decades. You are making a big decision that will dramatically influence where you will live and what you will study for the next four years of your life. Don't take that decision lightly, and don't base it on what colors you like best or how much you like watching sports.

Engage in a proper analysis of the university using variables that will matter to your career. These schools can be very helpful as a tool in your quest to live the life you were meant to live. At the same time, though, they can be overvalued based on variables that aren't important in the long run. Don't make that mistake.

Elite Institutions

Finally, we come to elite institutions. These are the Ivy League schools and a handful of other colleges and universities highly regarded in the very upper echelons of prestige. Only a small percentage of students will have the type of profile to get

152

into such a school. If this is you, you need to decide if it's worth it for you to attend an elite institution. There is no doubt you will receive a top-notch education. The question you need to ask yourself is whether that is the best choice for your future plans.

It all goes back to your *why*. What's your mission, and what type of job do you want to achieve after college? In some jobs, going to an elite institution will prove to be a very wise investment. In other professions, university prestige does little to advance your career. These are the types of issues you need to consider when deciding if an elite institution is the right place for you. The reality is, it's not always worth it to attend one of these top schools.

Elite institutions have been accused of not actually making students great. On the contrary, they have a reputation for cherry-picking students. Some argue these schools are great recruiters of students who have all the skills it takes to perform at a high level after college—meaning, those students would have done just fine with a lower-level college degree.

Malcolm Gladwell has spent the last decade examining research on students entering elite institutions. It's been his on-again-off-again hobby, it seems. He highlights that individuals who were accepted into elite institutions but chose not to go often perform just as well on a variety of post-college outcomes as those who went to the elite university. He went on to argue in his book *David and Goliath* that if you are on the margin, or if you just barely can make it into an elite school and would be at the bottom of your class once you arrive, it would actually be *better* for you to go to a lesser school. He argues that there is a lot of value in being a big fish in a small pond.

Ben here. I think I would have thrived being a big fish in a small pond. As I mentioned earlier, I applied to all the elite institutions because I knew being accepted would provide the validation I craved. I was accepted to New York University, where we're sometimes called the Harvard on the Hudson. The joke is that only people who went to NYU refer to NYU as the Harvard on the Hudson. It was an incredible school, I had an amazing experience, and I made relationships that I still value to this day.

However, I didn't go into that decision fully aware of what I was trying to accomplish. There were two things I didn't pay enough attention to when picking my college: community and coursework. As far as the community goes, the school couldn't have been more urban. There was no actual campus, only a network of buildings all over New York City. I had to take the subway to get to some of my classes! Further, the dorms were so expensive I lived in an apartment the first year with a high school friend who was also going to school in New York City. In a school of over 20,000 students, I felt extremely isolated. I was set adrift in this new experience after moving across the country, and it was difficult at times. Once I found my people on campus, I was set. This is true no matter where you go to school—the quicker you find a new community to experience school with, the more likely you are to be successful.

154

And let me tell you something, these new friends might not just walk into your life. This takes work, and it can be hard to really put yourself out there and meet new people, but the benefit is a much richer college experience.

I say I didn't pay enough attention to coursework because I didn't know what major to work toward. I had been so focused on getting into a school like NYU that I hadn't thought of what to study once I got there. And once I was there, I realized exactly how much I would be spending. Therefore, I didn't choose a major so much based on practicality but on what would get me through the quickest, so I could reduce the cost my parents would have to pay for college. This worked for me because the school I was accepted to at NYU allowed me to create my own major from all the courses NYU offered. Looking back on this experience, I recognize it was perfect for my situation, and I'm not only grateful to NYU but also incredibly proud of the degree I earned.

Reading this section, you might assume we're telling you that elite institutions don't have value. Of course they do, it's just a question of whether they have value for your particular situation and post-college goals. If you would like to be a politician, corporate lawyer, Wall Street broker, or a host of other such jobs, having an elite institution stamped on your diploma helps get you in the club. If you want to surround yourself with people who are brilliant and highly motivated, an elite institution is a great place, but don't think those same people can't be found at every type of school.

155

So, if you've set your sights on an elite institution, take your time, analyze your reasons, and be sure it's truly the best choice for your college and career goals.

Historically Black Colleges and Universities (HBCUs)

Do you remember in Chapter 1 we talked about how you should get college advice from people who actually know something about college? That isn't just talk. That's why we reached out to an expert to write this section on HBCUs. We have a lot of experience in a variety of college institutions, but it would be disingenuous to pretend to be experts on the benefits of HBCUs or the experience of a Black student in the current university system.

We reached out to Gabrielle Smith, PhD, to write this section. Gabrielle is a psychology professor at Texas Woman's University with an expertise in personality research. Her research examines how personality, race, and attitudes can influence perceptions and outcomes of college education, and she has both education and experience in HBCUs. She now conducts research on students attending HBCUs. Read her story below.

What are HBCUs? There are certain institutions that appeal to segments of the population historically excluded from higher education. Historically Black colleges or universities (HBCUs) were originally founded when individuals of African descent were barred from attending other institutions of higher learning. Largely situated in the southern region of the United States, approximately one hundred HBCUs exist today, and they remain the institution of choice for many students.

Specifically designed to foster the educational attainment for individuals with African heritage, HBCUs are often cited as a safe-haven for the Black intellectual experience. While only constituting around 3% of the nation's institutions, HBCUs account for a significant portion of African American doctors, lawyers, and PhD recipients.

Students at HBCUs are often allotted an education that centers the Black experience as an important part of their academic narrative. Many HBCUs require courses on African American history or the African Diaspora as central components of the general curriculum for all students. Thus, students are formally exposed to Black heritage early in their matriculation.

In addition to placing the Black experience at the forefront of the college narrative, HBCUs often have a higher retention and graduation rate for Black students compared to predominately white institutions (PWIs). HBCUs often boast a climate of social justice and a commitment to producing conscientious leaders for a more just society. Socially speaking, students at HBCUs are often a part of the majority in a way that is not normally the case in the larger social context. Unique culturally centered approaches to social experiences, such as Greek life and homecoming, make the social life at an HBCU vastly different from those at other colleges.

HBCUs usually have lower endowments than their PWI counterparts, making them less likely to have some of the resources that some PWI institutions have. However, HBCUs are often revered for the ability to produce competitive scholars with limited resources. Thus, it is important to understand what amenities you want your chosen institution to have and ensure that access is available.

If you are not a student of African descent, but find that an HBCU would potentially be a great fit, do not exclude yourself from the possibility. HBCUs do cater to students with African ancestry, however, they are quickly becoming more racially and ethnically diverse. "Historically Black" should not be conflated with "only Black," as HBCUs admit students regardless of their racial and ethnic backgrounds. While many of these schools are still majority Black institutions, students from varying ethnic backgrounds are now choosing to attend HBCUs, and there are even a few HBCUs that have majority non-Black student enrollment.

While HBCUs share the common thread of centering the Black experience to the educational pursuits of their students, individual institutions diverge on an array of academic components. Thus, if you are interested in an HBCU experience, you may want to refer to other sections in this book to help you decide what type of HBCU you'd like to attend. Depending on your intended major, you may want to pinpoint the HBCUs that are known for areas related to your interests. While exploring your options of HBCUs, determine the components of the experience that appeal to you. Investigate all institutions on your list to see which would potentially meet your diversified needs as a student.

My experience at an HBCU women's college. I was a first-generation college student unsure about everything, including my abilities. However, when I first stepped foot on Spelman College's campus, I felt at home. I didn't want to go or be anywhere else. I felt like I instantly belonged and couldn't wait to be a part of this Black sisterhood.

Prior to attending Spelman, I had been the only or one of the only students of color in my high school AP classes. My four years at Spelman were amazing. The ability to simultaneously center the Black woman's experiences *and* be unique in my expression and representation of Black womanhood was liberating. I was allowed so much time and space to focus on my education without being concerned about how or why I fit, because I naturally fit in and matched the description of the typical Spelman student. I felt nurtured by faculty and was inundated with examples of faculty members who looked like me and were successful in the domains that I deemed important.

Spelman expanded my dreams. As a high school student, I never thought about anything beyond a bachelor's degree, but by sophomore year, I imagined the possibilities above and beyond undergraduate education. Now I am a professor with a PhD in psychology and am striving to be a promoter of dreaming big for my students, as faculty at Spelman were for me.

Now What?

I hope you found this overview helpful. Now that you know the options available to you, can you see one or several potential paths forward? As you read through the options, which type of college resonated with you? Will you thrive as a big fish in a small pond? Will an Ivy League education set you up for the kind of post-college network you need? Can community college courses give you that jumping-off point to your four-year college?

We have developed a short assessment tool designed to help you decide what type of college experience makes the most sense for your situation. This is our gift to you for purchasing and reading this book. You can find the assessment at www.unbrandedstudent.com/collegetype.

Your decision is complex and personal. This assessment won't give you the perfect answer for every situation, but it can help you get started in making a plan.

This book is all about empowering you to make an informed choice for your college search. You're almost to the end! Are you ready to take the final step of writing your story?

7 Go Forth

It's time to go forth and continue your journey. You're stepping out with more tools in your box. You've learned about yourself, your dreams, and the options waiting for you in the world of college. The final step is to embrace the unknown.

The unknown? Wait, I thought this was all about fact-finding and making informed choices.

That's true. But there's also a huge dose of ambiguity in the years ahead of you, and we wouldn't be serving you well if we ignored that reality. So, before we send you off, we want to talk about skill sets you can cultivate to get you through the uncertainties ahead.

Whatever your strengths, your passions, and the mission that drives you, understand that your road to meaning, fulfillment, greatness, or whatever you want to call the destination won't be a straight line. This road will have bumps, it will have twists, and there will be roadblocks along the way. For those of you who went through the online course, this is why we worked together to write a life mission statement. This articulation of your passions, your inner *why*, is going to help you power through these obstacles on your path.

I hope you're looking at your college search full of optimism, promise, and confidence. You should. Find the things that fan that flame and encourage your hopes and dreams, so that when challenges come, you don't lose sight of where you're going.

When I (Ben) graduated from NYU, I had a vague sense of my *why*. Like I've told you before, my entire focus was to go to the biggest branded university that would have me. And as you know, dear reader, I couldn't possibly know what job or major that would have led to. My hope was to start a business ... without any experience. I was hoping to move to Vietnam and do something huge. It's fine to dream big. It's also fine to be flexible enough to have contingency plans so that when life pivots, it doesn't seem like the end of the world.

Don't let hardship derail you. And don't let your focus, your dream, your passion become so all-consuming and essential that you can't adapt to the unforeseen but inevitable changes of life. It is highly likely that your job in twenty years doesn't even exist now. But if you know what direction you are headed, and you have developed valuable skills in those fields, you will be ready to transition and maneuver in a changing job market.

Paying Your Dues

My path after college started with selling mini-vans in the suburbs of Dallas to really nice families. I was distraught when I started that job. What self-respecting NYU graduate in all the history of NYU ever went back to live with his parents to sell cars? I'm pretty sure no one has done the research, but I'm guessing it's less than five people. But you know what? I'm not doing that now. That was one small twist in my story, but looking back, I can see how important it was in helping me grow to be the person I am now. I learned things during that time I hadn't learned anywhere else; honestly, I don't think I could have learned them anywhere else.

That twist was an enormous time of growth and learning for me. It sucks that oftentimes we have to deal with challenges or changes to our carefully laid plans, but this is where personal growth happens. During that time selling cars, I learned humility. I learned the brand of my college wasn't nearly as important as I wanted it to be. Most importantly, I learned to sell. NYU instilled in me a love for learning. The car dealership taught me my passion for sales. When I tell people I'm in sales, they often respond by telling me how much they hate sales. They hate it because it's hard, the hardest thing we have to do—and we have to do it every day. Everything you do is selling. If you aren't selling a product, you're selling an idea to your team, or yourself to an employer, or a plan to your spouse. The task of sales never ends.

I couldn't see it then, but that time in my life was teaching me, molding me, growing me. It prepared me for the next thing, the next job. Then, I moved on to the next opportunity, and I learned valuable lessons there, and I refined my passion and my mission. Then I moved on to the next job or phase of my life. And on and on it goes.

You might be nodding your head and thinking, *Yeah, that makes sense.* But let me tell you, when you're working your first or second or third job that's not your dream job, it doesn't feel like it makes sense. Sometimes it's hard to do something that feels like a daily grind. Sometimes you wonder if you're wasting your time. Sometimes you ask what it's all for. That's okay. It's natural. It's called *paying your dues.*

You've heard of that, right? It means doing the hard things you don't love because you're learning the lessons, gaining the skills, and mastering the expertise that pave the way to the dream job. Almost no one goes from college to dream job. That's just not how it works. Because no one picks up a paintbrush and is immediately a Picasso. No swimmer jumps in the pool and is an instant Michael Phelps. You put in your time, do the hard work, and run the drills until you're experienced, intuitive, and well-connected enough that the hard things become second nature and you're naturally ready to move to the next level and the next after that.

During that time, do your best to embrace the process. Find a way to keep dreaming and have faith that the hard work isn't wasted, it isn't forever; it's a few steps along the road to achieving your dreams, to finding and living your mission. But keep your head up, continue to acquire valuable skills, and be ready to pivot when new opportunities come your way.

What I'm trying to say here is: you will evolve over time. When you start out, you work the logistics, and you volunteer for the big stuff, and as you grow in your career the pendulum swings so that you gain expertise and get paid to do more of the things you love.

Speaking of Skills ...

I told you that everyone is selling something every day. In the same way, there are other attributes all students need to cultivate as they go through the college experience. These are critical to every person's success. While this book's focus is to help you make the correct college choice, we want you to succeed while you're there and beyond. So in this final chapter, we share with you a short rundown of some skill sets and characteristics you should refine during your college years to help you succeed.

Be a Risk-Taker

You need to learn how to take calculated risks in life. We aren't advising recklessness, but many people are too passive; they just let life happen to them. There are times when you need to do things that take some faith. Being a risk-taker can help in many domains. It might not have to be what characterizes your future—you don't have to be an entrepreneur or a stunt double—but it can help to fuel your professional growth.

A great way to train your risk muscle it to engage in a side hustle in your free time; begin experimenting with businesses on the side. If business isn't your thing, think of joining community projects that address an issue you're passionate about.

When you start something, you get to be the leader—that just happens by default. With so many people in your high school and college community, the opportunities to lead are limited. But if you start something, you are the de facto leader. This provides invaluable experience and an incredible talking point when you start the interview process upon graduation.

In *The $100 Start Up*, Chris Guillebeau talks about how a side hustle can change your life. The key to the approach is to keep it reasonable at first. I wanted to start a business in Vietnam to help Vietnamese students find their place at American universities. Maybe I should have started with application coaching via email from America while I was a junior and senior in college, rather than going all in and planning to move to Vietnam.

Maybe starting something new isn't for you. That doesn't get you out of learning to take risks. Any time you apply for a new job, learn a new skill, or do anything outside of your comfort zone you are taking a risk. Some of us are so passive and willing to work within an established system that we have forgotten what it means to take a risk. Use college as a chance to build your risk muscle back up. If you see an opportunity, go for it! Even if it is a long shot. If you want to try a club or a

166

class or something else, do it! You'll either succeed and be able to do something new, or you'll fail and realize that taking a risk and failing really isn't that bad.

Be a Campaigner

Some people are true believers by nature, and they don't mind telling others what they believe. Whether this is about a belief system, a set of policies, or a product, it takes a missional attitude and disregard of rejection to go out day after day into the world and not be afraid to be told no again and again—all for that one yes.

Some people have a personality that enables them to campaign for themselves. This doesn't come naturally for the rest of us. If that's true for you, you'll need to be intentional about cultivating that skill.

How do you do that? Pay attention to what you're good at and not good at. Practice bragging on yourself in essays, applications, and interviews. This is the one time it's not good to be humble or shy about your accomplishments. Be willing to sell yourself to your potential college and your future employer. Now, you also want the skills and talents to back it up, and you don't want your self-promotion campaign to go overboard. Too much passion without enough structure is a killer. The best part of having a campaigner inside you is that if you can survive the struggles of youth and find a way to channel this passion when you hit your thirties, there is great reward.

If you're not able to stick up for yourself and to take credit for your hard work, try to develop that. Just like sales isn't only for the sales division of a company, these attributes of a post-college lifestyle are something we all have to develop. It might just make the difference in whether you stand out above your competitors.

Be a Communicator

Learning to communicate well is a skill multiplier. Having strong communication skills is valuable in and of itself, but an often-overlooked advantage is that it allows your other traits to shine. You are going to college to develop skills valuable to your industry and future profession, but if you cannot clearly communicate your value to others, you'll have a hard time getting your foot in the door.

But it doesn't stop there. Not only does communication make it easier to land the job in the industry you want, it fuels your growth in the day-to-day responsibilities on the job. You will likely start your career in the weeds doing the more basic work, but as you move up, you might be leading projects and groups of people. As a result, your ability to communicate and the value of your communication skills increase over time.

There are two key channels you must master: written communication and verbal communication.

Learn to write clearly and efficiently. You don't have to use Steinbeckian prose, but you need to be able to

168

communicate your point clearly with minimal errors. Most offices aren't expecting perfection, but they need proficiency.

You also need to be able to speak effectively. No one expects you to be an entertainer or the life of the party if that isn't your personality, but you should be able to have a conversation with a peer, supervisor, or subordinate and communicate effectively in each scenario. You should also be able to get in front of a small group and present your work. If this freaks you out, the best solution is to practice. You will get practice in school. If you need more, look for a local Toastmasters group. Remember to focus on proficiency and not perfection. This should decrease your fear of failure and lower the pressure you put on yourself.

Be Emotionally Intelligent

Some people do everything by the book, but they stall out in their career because they cannot operate well in an organization. If you have ever been around little kids, you know they sometimes cry and scream when they don't get their way. That's fine, they are kids. But, unfortunately, we all know thirty-, forty-, and fifty-year-olds who throw a fit when they don't get their way. This is a sign of poor emotional intelligence. These adults have almost certainly missed out on promotions because of their behavior—even if they had the competence to do the job.

Another piece of emotional intelligence is having the ability to interact appropriately with other people. Put your phone down and work on your ability to have a conversation. Listen to others! It is important that as you go through your college career you make a conscious effort to improve your self-awareness, self-regulation (self-control), empathy, self-motivation, and social skills. These skills are difficult to put on a résumé, but they are key in obtaining people in your life who are willing to champion you and root for your success.

You won't become emotionally intelligent overnight; it's something you develop by consistent and intentional practice. Carol Dweck, a leading researcher in the field of motivation, has spent her career championing this concept, which she calls *growth mindset*. Growth mindset arises from what neuroscience teaches us about the brain. The idea is that because your brain is malleable, you are able to improve tasks or skills through hard work. The reason not everyone benefits from this is that you have to *believe it* and *practice it* to see the results; it's a self-fulfilling prophesy.

Decide what kinds of changes you'd like to see in the realm of your emotional intelligence, set goals, and develop intentional practices to reach those goals. You'll see significant changes in no time.

Be Efficient and Effective

Another foundational skill you need to learn is how to prioritize work and then how to get that work done efficiently. This is not a new idea, but mastering it will provide outsized returns in your college career, your job, and your adult life.

When you are ready to sit down to work on your coursework, how do you know what to work on?

The first thing you need to do is determine what is most important. Sometimes this is driven by deadlines. At other times, you prioritize by asking: What project or idea will be most impactful for me? There are many books you can read to help you tease this out, but be *thoughtful* about what you are doing. Most students do not approach study, or even school, with much of a plan. They sit down at the library and just start to "study," but they don't really know what that means. Pareto's Law, also known as the 80/20 Rule, states that 80% of our results come from 20% of our actions. Find your most impactful 20% and be sure that you're spending some time to focus on these tasks each day. When you study, part of this 20% should include active recall. Don't just read your book or notes, put them away and see if you can simplify them in your mind and explain them to a novice. If you can't, you aren't ready yet. This practice alone is more helpful than rereading your textbook five times.

Figuring out which tasks to engage in is foundational to success, but once you have done that, you need to determine the best way to complete those important tasks. This is the skill of efficiency. There are a variety of techniques available to help you develop efficiency. Some of these might be as simple as the Pomodoro Technique. With this approach, you work a twenty-five-minute session (or whatever time frame you find most productive) followed by a five-minute break. After several rounds, you take a longer break to recharge.

There are other, more-complicated options out there as well. Some people create entire systems to organize their tasks and plan out how to complete them. The most famous of these comes from David Allen's book *Getting Things Done*, often referred to as GTG by dedicated followers. This approach is more complicated and needs a full reading of the book to be implemented, but it's based on having all your tasks written down and an actionable plan for completing them. This will leave your mind free to complete the work; you are no longer using your mental horsepower to manage your to-do list in your head. These are two popular methods, but there are many more.

Lots of people debate which methods are most effective, but the important point is that you find a system that works for you, one you can stick with. When it's time to work, you do so in a thoughtful manner, focusing on the most important tasks and completing them efficiently. If you can do this, you will set yourself up for success in college and in your future career.

Be Deep

Focusing deeply on a subject or task for a long stretch of time day after day is a skill that must be cultivated. Mason Currey's interesting book, *Daily Rituals*, highlights the lives of creatives, scientists, and other historical figures who accomplished great things. One commonality you see among their profiles is a commitment to their craft. Successful people across industries all shared this one ability: dedication to daily focused routines and processes that advanced their work.

It is clear that some people are more naturally inclined to this focused work than others. Autistic savants, for example, can remain engrossed in their work for hours at a time, often so highly focused that they cannot be distracted by the world around them. However, you don't have to be born with it. You can attain advanced knowledge of a subject or achieve world-class artistic abilities through hours of deliberate practice in your discipline. If this kind of focus doesn't come naturally to you, it's okay; cultivate this skill over time, one step at a time.

In his book *The Shallows*, Nicholas Carr dives deep into the science behind the way our digital environment is changing our brains. The implications are scary. We should all be more mindful of how we use our devices to soothe every ounce of boredom we feel. The overstimulation of smartphones and other digital devices is rewiring our brains, and we are now so used to immediate feedback and updates that many of us are no longer able to focus and concentrate for an extended period of time.

In *Deep Work*, Cal Newport argues that the ability to focus deeply is so rare in our current culture that learning to cultivate this skill can pay outsized dividends in the marketplace. And this is happening at a time when most high-paying jobs in our economy require deep thought for success! Developing the ability to focus deeply can set you apart from the crowd and allow you to perform better at work in less time. Learning to focus can increase your productivity to a point where you may actually be able to work fewer hours to achieve the same amount of output.

This carries over to studying. An hour of intense focus on a subject is better than three or four hours of study time interrupted by chats, texts, and Facebook checks. Focusing on depth is a skill that must be cultivated. Use your time in college to train your brain to focus during your study time. Put your phone away. This will pay dividends both in class and your career.

There are whole books dedicated to exploring each of the skills we've outlined above. We haven't given you a full how-to on succeeding in college and career, but if you take a thoughtful approach to these skills, you will be well ahead of the game. Did any of these skills resonate with you? Go deeper. Check out a book or a podcast on the subject. Start practicing now, and think intentionally about how to make those practices part of your lifestyle. That's what *paying your dues* is all about. One small step at a time. Persistence and perseverance. And a giant dose of faith to believe all those steps are paving a path to the future you dream of.

A Modern-day Dreamer

Elon Musk has a dream to put humans on Mars, and if the track record of his company, SpaceX, is any indication, he'll see that dream realized in your lifetime. And it all started right after he graduated from Stanford University … right?

Wrong.

In fact, he didn't make it to graduation. He arrived at Stanford at the start of the Internet boom, so he dropped out within his first week to be part of it! Instead of attending school, he launched his first company, Zip2 Corporation.[28]

After selling Zip2 in 1999, Musk co-founded X.com, which later became PayPal.

Then in 2002, SpaceX was born. The company intended to build spacecraft for commercial space travel. But it almost failed. By the final trial of their first rocket, they were out of money; they had one more chance. Fortunately, it worked, and from that point on they attracted investors and national attention. By 2008, NASA took notice and contracted the company to transport cargo to the International Space Station.

The company made history in 2017 with the successful test flight and landing of the first reusable rocket. *Reusable rocket.* You might not be an expert in rocket science, but this is a huge deal; it is essentially the next step required to send normal people like us to the moon, or Mars, or Hogwarts. If you haven't seen the video of this rocket landing, Google it right now. This technology is going to revolutionize space travel. And it has made Musk's dream of putting humans on Mars a real possibility.

---

[28] "Elon Musk Biography," Biography.com, updated February 9, 2018, www.biography.com/people/elon-musk-20837159.

Elon Musk is also well known for his groundbreaking work with electric cars, battery products, and solar roof tiles. But this empire has taken him decades to build. He wasn't working on going to Mars fresh out of college in 1999, yet he might just put humans on the red planet within the next few decades! This is the power of hard work, dedication, and a tireless belief in a dream. This is the advantage of paying your dues.

Elon Musk knows his mission. Do you know yours? Can you hold onto your vision of the future with every small step it takes to get there? Imagine how you might shape the world with that kind of outlook.

Go Forth

You've done what we've asked of you. You've discovered your talents, skills, aptitudes, and passions. You have an eye on your mission. You're charting a course to college and beyond. You've kept your end of the bargain. Have we kept ours? Have we helped you write a new story—your story? Maybe the answer lies in you. In the telling of your story. We hope and trust it's going to be a good one.

THE
UNBRANDED STUDENT
ONLINE COURSE

Ready to Reclaim Your College Search?

Understand who you are and pick the best school for you!

Our five-week course will guide you through the process of analyzing your strengths and evaluating your college options. We will teach you what you need to know about the college decision-making process and walk you through developing a short list of schools that best fit you and your situation.

Find out more at www.unbrandedstudent.com/course.

PARTNER WITH US
Bring UNBRANDED to Your School

Bad college advice hurts students, and it's everywhere. We want to help your students avoid bad college advice—especially the idea that they are a brand.

Your students are more than a brand.

Yes, even while the world says otherwise. Today's social media environment has turned teens into brand managers, responsible for constructing an image for the world to see, like, and share. Guiding your students in the college-selection process has never felt more daunting; choosing the right brand, never more important. It's our job to ensure our students know they are more than the letters on a sweatshirt or colors in a crest. They are individuals. Their gifts, interests, learning styles, and ambitions deserve careful consideration. That's what we're here for: to provide the tools to help your students select a college that will support the vision they have for their life.

The Unbranded Student **book and online course will empower your students to:**

1. Articulate what makes them special.

2. Understand what college can—and can't—do for their future.

3. Formulate a thoughtful and actionable college-selection process.

We help students create a college-search strategy that makes sense for who they are, not who they think a college wants them to be.

We want to partner with your school. Students of partner schools gain access to *The Unbranded Student* online course at significantly discounted prices. To learn more about partnering with us to serve your students, contact us at www.unbrandedstudent.com/partners or email us at info@unbrandedstudent.com.

ACKNOWLEDGMENTS

We want to acknowledge everyone who supported this project. From our wives and our children, who love us unconditionally; to our editor, who worked diligently to make this book what is has become; to our parents, who were so selfless during our own college search.

RESOURCES

Personality Inventory

Myers-Briggs

To take a Myers-Briggs test and read about your type, start here: www.mbtionline.com/TaketheMBTI.

Visit PsychCentral for a free version: https://psychcentral.com/quizzes/personality/start.php.

Enneagram

To get a detailed overview of the Enneagram and find your type, start with The Enneagram Institute at www.enneagraminstitute.com. There are also many great books and podcasts that go deeper into the Enneagram approach, just use your Google.

Big Five

To learn more about the Big Five personality traits model and take a test, visit www.mindtools.com/pages/article/newCDV_22.htm.

CliftonStrengths

To read more about CliftonStrengths, visit the website at gallupstrengthscenter.com. There is a great book written by Buckingham and Clifton specifically for students called *CliftonStrengths for Students*.

Unbranded Resources

For more information about the Myers-Briggs, the Enneagram, or the Big Five, you can also visit our website at www.unbrandedstudent.com. There you'll find links and resources to guide you in your attempt to better understand how you are wired.

You can find *The Unbranded Brief: Student Personality Profile* and *The Unbranded College Search Matrix* for free at www.unbrandedstudent.com/resources.

Research Tools

Bureau of Labor Statistics: You'll find a wide variety of topics covered on the bureau's website, including employment, wages, and various industry data.

Institute for College Access & Success (TICAS): The TICAS website is a great place to research student debt and financial aid at both the national level and the state level.

Integrated Postsecondary Education Data System (IPEDS): IPEDS conducts research and provides data on postsecondary students, faculty, staff, and resources. You can find a wealth of information on their website about graduation rates, student enrollment, financial aid availability, and much more.

The College Scorecard: The college scorecard is a great way to access college information collected by the U.S. Department of Education. Here is where you can find information on the average cost of attendance, average debt at graduation, and average first-year salary for alumni.

BIBLIOGRAPHY

"Blake Mycoskie." TOMS. www.toms.com/blakes-bio.

Burrows, Brianna. "What is a Community College in the USA?"
studyusa.com. Accessed February 25, 2018.
https://studyusa.com/en/a/1236/what-is-a-
community-college-in-the-usa.

Camera, Lauren. "Study: Students Rely on Least Reliable Source
for Advice on College Majors." *U.S. News & World
Report*. September 25, 2017.
www.usnews.com/news/education-
news/articles/2017-09-25/students-rely-on-least-
reliable-source-for-advice-on-college-majors-friends-
and-family?src=usn_tw.

Carter, Shawn M. "Here's what happens if you default on your
student loans—and how to get back on track."
CNBC.com. October 9, 2017.
www.cnbc.com/2017/10/09/what-happens-and-what-
to-do-if-you-default-on-a-student-loan.html.

Copeland, Jack. "Alan Turing: The codebreaker who saved
'millions of lives.'" BBC.com. June 19, 2012.
www.bbc.com/news/technology-18419691.

DiGangi, Christine. "The average student loan debt in every
state." *USA Today*. April 28, 2017.
www.usatoday.com/story/money/personalfinance/20
17/04/28/average-student-loan-debt-every-
state/100893668/.

"Dropping Out, Again: Why So Many College Students Never Graduate." NBCNews.com. November 18, 2014. www.nbcnews.com/news/education/dropping-out-again-why-so-many-college-students-never-graduate-n246956.

Durando, Jessica. "10 inspiring quotes by Mother Teresa." *USA Today*. August 26, 2014. www.usatoday.com/story/news/nation-now/2014/08/26/mother-teresa-quotes/14364401/.

"Elon Musk Biography." Biography.com. Updated February 9, 2018. www.biography.com/people/elon-musk-20837159.

Fain, Paul. "Second Thoughts About Higher Education Decisions." Inside Higher Ed. June 1, 2017. www.insidehighered.com/news/2017/06/01/survey-finds-regrets-among-most-former-college-students-belief-quality-their.

Frankl, Viktor E. *Man's Search for Meaning*. Boston: Beacon Press, 2006.

Grant, Adam. *Originals: How Non-Conformists Move the World*. New York: Penguin Random House, 2016.

"I Know Why the Caged Bird Sings Quotes." Goodreads.com. Accessed February 3, 2018. www.goodreads.com/work/quotes/1413589-i-know-why-the-caged-bird-sings.

Kolodner, Meredith. "Why are graduation rates at community colleges so low?" The Hechinger Report. May 5, 2015.

http://hechingerreport.org/new-book-addresses-low-community-college-graduation-rates/.

Longley, Robert. "Lifetime Earnings Soar with Education." ThoughtCo. June 4, 2017. www.thoughtco.com/lifetime-earnings-soar-with-education-3321730.

Marcus, Jon. "Universities and colleges struggle to stem big drops in enrollment." The Hechinger Report. June 29, 2017. http://hechingerreport.org/universities-colleges-struggle-stem-big-drops-enrollment/.

"'MBTI® Basics." The Myers & Briggs Foundation. Accessed February 15, 2018. www.myersbriggs.org/my-mbti-personality-type/mbti-basics/home.htm?bhcp=1.

NSC Research Center. "Signature 14 Completing College: A National View of Student Completion Rates—Fall 2011 Cohort." December 13, 2017. https://nscresearchcenter.org/signaturereport14/.

"Personality." American Psychological Association. Accessed March 4, 2018. www.apa.org/topics/personality/index.aspx.

Scott-Clayton, Judith. "The looming student loan default crisis is worse than we thought." Brookings. January 11, 2018. www.brookings.edu/research/the-looming-student-loan-default-crisis-is-worse-than-we-thought/.

"Which traits predict job performance?" American Psychological Association. Accessed February 15,

2018. www.apa.org/helpcenter/predict-job-performance.aspx.

Made in the USA
Columbia, SC
04 May 2020